BURT FRANKLIN: RESEARCH & SOURCE WORKS SERIES
Theater & Drama Series 29

THE PLOT AND ITS CONSTRUCTION
IN
EIGHTEENTH CENTURY CRITICISM
OF FRENCH COMEDY

THE PLOT AND ITS CONSTRUCTION
IN
EIGHTEENTH CENTURY CRITICISM
OF FRENCH COMEDY

A STUDY OF THEORY
WITH RELATION TO
THE PRACTICE OF BEAUMARCHAIS

A DISSERTATION

PRESENTED TO THE FACULTY OF BRYN MAWR COLLEGE IN
PARTIAL FULFILLMENT OF THE REQUIREMENTS
FOR THE DEGREE OF DOCTOR OF PHILOSOPHY

BY

EDNA C. FREDRICK

BURT FRANKLIN
New York, N. Y.

Published by LENOX HILL Pub. & Dist. Co. (Burt Franklin)
235 East 44th St., New York, N.Y. 10017
Reprinted: 1973
Printed in the U.S.A.

Burt Franklin: Research and Source Works Series
Theater and Drama Series 29

Reprinted from the original edition in the Bryn Mawr College
    Library.

Library of Congress Cataloging in Publication Data

Fredrick, Edna Caroline, 1906-
    The plot and its construction in eighteenth century criticism
of French comedy.

Thesis—Bryn Mawr.
Vita.
Reprint of the 1934 ed.
Bibliography: p.
    1. Plots (Drama, novel, etc.) 2. French drama—18th century—History
and criticism. 3. French drama (Comedy)—History and criticism. 4. Beau-
marchais, Pierre Augustin Caron de, 1732-1799. I. Title.
PQ538.F7 1973   842'.052   72-82001
ISBN 0-8337-4118-7

ACKNOWLEDGMENT

I wish to express here my gratitude to Dr. Helen E. Patch, Professor of French at Mount Holyoke College, to whose inspiring teaching I owe my first interest in French Literature and who gave me many helpful suggestions when I was writing the first part of this dissertation in Paris.

It is also a pleasure for me to acknowledge my indebtedness to M. Paul Hazard of the Collège de France under whose direction I worked while in Paris and whose assistance and guidance were of inestimable value; without them my work could not have been accomplished.

Above all, I wish in a very special manner to thank Dr. Eunice Morgan Schenck of Bryn Mawr College who, during my years of graduate study, has been a constant source of encouragement and inspiration. My chief work has been done under her direction and it was she who suggested to me the subject of this dissertation.

TABLE OF CONTENTS

INTRODUCTION

The first quarter of the nineteenth century witnessed the phenomenal triumph of the "pièce bien faite." The master in this *genre* at the beginning of the century was Eugène Scribe; from his time on, a substantial plot, developed with irreproachable technique, became the *sine qua non* of every theatrical success. While it would be absurd to deny that it was the imprint of his dramatic genius which fixed the "rules" of the art, it is equally absurd to maintain that Scribe created a demand and did not respond to one already existent.

In the years immediately preceding the popularity of Scribe, Andrieux describes thus the effect which the performance of classical comedy had upon the contemporary audience:

> Que de critiques sur les invraisemblances, sur les inconvenances! Souffrirait-on les confidences qui se font dans la rue ou sur une place publique, *Arnolphe* y amenant *Agnès* pour la sermonner, et le juge *Bartholin* venant y tenir audience? Que dirait-on des entrées et des sorties sans motifs, et des dénouemens qui se font par la substitution d'un papier à un autre, par la surprise d'une signature! etc., (*sic*) Tout cela n'engage à rien, si ce n'est devant un notaire de comédie; ces dénouemens postiches ne satisferaient point nos spectateurs, devenus plus difficiles sur la vérité de l'action, comme sur toutes les autres parties de l'art.[1]

It is possible to consider this demand for more perfect dramatic technique the result of the work of Beaumarchais. The example of Beaumarchais, however, does not fully explain the observation made by Andrieux, for, in the period intervening between Scribe and Beaumarchais, Beaumarchais' genius as a dramatic technician seems to have been singularly overlooked by contemporary critics.[2]

A curious fact, the significance of which has perhaps not been

---

[1] Andrieux, *Oeuvres,* 1822, v. 1, p. 222. Preface to 1808 edition of the play.

[2] Andrieux himself accords him no importance in tracing the evolution of comedy and what he terms its "renaissance" at the end of the eighteenth century. "Beaumarchais avait donné avec un très grand succès qui se soutient encore, son *Barbier de Séville,* comédie fort jolie et fort spirituelle; mais cet auteur très-original ne pouvait guère être imité: son comique est à lui, et à lui seul." (*Oeuvres,* 1818–1823, v. 4, p. 22, n. 1.) Duval, one of the most suc-

sufficiently emphasized,[3] indicates that Beaumarchais himself marked the culmination rather than the beginning of a new conception of comedy. *Le Barbier de Séville* was not originally presented to the public of 1775 in the perfect form in which we know it; Beaumarchais, consumed with a desire for satirical vengeance, had sprinkled his original version with large doses of sardonic wit and increased the original four-act draft to a five-act play.[4] It is natural to suppose that Beaumarchais' inimitable *esprit* would conceal, or at least compensate for, the resultant defects in the composition of the play and that this super-abundance of wit would be a guarantee for its success. On the contrary, however, the five-act play met with immediate disapproval and it was not until Beaumarchais had reduced it in form to the original version that the public was willing to accept his comedy. Apparently the audience of 1775 was as determined as the one described by Andrieux in 1808 to refuse an old, familiar plot unless it were presented in a new and more perfect form. No more than Scribe was Beaumarchais creating a demand. He, also, was responding to one which was already existent; he himself was the product of an anterior development which had by the end of the eighteenth century gained sufficient momentum to be carried along by its own force until the advent of Scribe.

It is my aim to trace this development which culminated in the work of Beaumarchais; to determine as closely as possible the time and the circumstances in which the plot of a comedy ceased to be considered merely incidental, as it was in the great plays of Molière, and became instead an integral and essential part of every good play. The method here adopted consists of a critical analysis of the theory of the period as it is expressed by the authors themselves in the prefaces and prologues to their comedies, in practical treatises dealing with dramatic art and in the criticism of contemporary comedies found in the periodicals, memoirs, literary and private correspondence of the time. It should be stated at the outset that it is not my purpose to present a history of the *comédie d'in-*

---

cessful authors of the period, fails to mention him in his numerous prefaces while Geoffroy, the most important critic of the period, contents himself with a polemic against the political and social aspects of Beaumarchais' comedies. (*Cours de littérature dramatique*, 1825, v. 5, pp. 408 f., *passim.*)

[3] Lintilhac, *Beaumarchais et ses oeuvres*, 1887, p. 251.

[4] Lintilhac, *op. cit.*, pp. 251–253.

trigue as such for this *genre* receives attention only in so far as it influenced other kinds of comedy, only in the measure in which it was admitted into other types of plays.

It may seem that a study of the values assigned to plot and its construction in the theory of eighteenth century comedy, wholly divorced from the practice of the period, is devoid of any importance, that comedy has no real meaning, no real existence apart from its representation on the stage. It is equally true, however, that of the seventy-odd authors read during the course of this study only three are remembered today, of the hundreds of plays written during the century only two comedies of Beaumarchais, a few of Marivaux and one, possibly two, of Regnard still enjoy real existence in the theatrical sense of the word and only a very few of all the others are still readable. Except for Beaumarchais, the century had little dramatic talent. Its genius expressed itself in theory. Diderot is the classic example. He wrote two comedies, *drames* if one prefers, which have little intrinsic value, but the ideas expressed in his *De la Poésie dramatique* explain in part the nineteenth century theater.

It should not be inferred from this exclusive attention to a single *genre* that the comedy of the period was pursuing an independent line of development. On the contrary, this study is concerned with but one manifestation of a fairly wide-spread interest in plot and its construction, an interest which is apparent in *genres* other than comedy. As early as 1708 Crébillon said of a tragedy: "J'aime mieux encore avoir chargé mon sujet d'épisodes que de déclamations."[5] In 1758 Piron wrote in greater detail in the preface to his tragedy, *Gustave Wasa:*

> La multiplicité des événemens, sans contredit, est inéxcusable, quand elle affoiblit, qu'elle exténuë, et qu'elle absorbe l'intérêt principal; quand elle est mal amenée, mal tissuë et mal débroüillé. . . . Mais si, au contraire, tous ces événemens procèdent sans peine les uns des autres, et se succèdent par une progression immédiate; s'ils s'entrelâssent et se démêlent avec ordre et sans embarras; si toujours subordonnés à l'action principale, ils ne font, en conduisant à la catastrophe, que la suspendre agréablement; . . . reprocher l'abondance alors, je le crois pouvoir dire,

[5] Cited by Gaiffe, *le Drame en France au XVIIIe siècle*, 1910, p. 452.

c'est mauvaise humeur; peut-être mauvaise foi; dirai-je même ingratitude? . . .

D'abord, à l'oüir, la multiplicité telle que je l'ai définie plus haût, renfermée avec clarté et précision dans l'unité d'intrigue, devroit bien (du moins quant à la difficulté surmontée) aller de pair en mérite, avec la simplicité soutenuë du charme seul de l'élégance et de l'harmonie. Est-il donc moins difficile, dit-elle, d'arranger des faits, que des mots? . . . Qu'il décide en effet dans lequel des deux, ou d'un Plan habilement compliqué, ou d'un amas de beaux vers, se trouve le plus de difficultés à vaincre; et de laquelle de ces deux sortes de difficultés vaincuës, le Théâtre tire un meilleur parti.[6]

In 1746 Riccoboni wrote in his *Discours sur la parodie* the following curious, but extremely interesting justification of the parody on the grounds of its superior construction:

Ils voudroient dans leurs Préfaces faire envisager une Parodie comme un morceau qui n'a d'autre mérite que de ressembler à la Piece dont elle est, disent-ils, une copie boufonne. Il y a un peu d'injustice dans cette façon d'exposer les choses. Une Parodie est souvent beaucoup mieux construite que l'Original. On y retranche du plan de l'Ouvrage toutes les Scênes de remplissage inutiles à l'action, dont les Tragédies abondent furieusement de nos jours . . .[7]

In an apology for the *opéra-bouffon* Nougaret leads one to conclude that the form of the *comédie mêlée d'ariettes,* the least regular of comedies, deserves some attention: ". . . je serais charmé . . . d'avoir prouvé que la Comédie-mêlée d'Ariettes est susceptible de toutes les règles, puisqu'on l'appelle un Drame."[8] And a year later in the preface to an *opéra-comique* Cailhava wrote in a not unsimilar, although perhaps more mocking, tone of this contemporary desire to give regularity to originally irregular dramatic forms:

Les Partisans de l'Opéra-comique sont divisés en deux classes. Ceux de la premiere, gâtés par Panard, par Vadé, par le célebre M. Favard, pensent que les Pieces de ce genre, enfants de la gaieté et d'une aimable négligence, doivent être regardées comme des bagatelles. Ceux de la

---

[6] Piron, *Oeuvres,* 1758, v. 2, pp. 38–54, *passim.*
[7] Romagnesi and Riccoboni, *Théâtre italien,* 1746, pp. 47–48.
[8] *De l'Art du théâtre,* 1769, Discours préliminaire, p. xiv.

seconde classe écrivent, et disent gravement: Qu'une petite montre, contenant autant de ressorts qu'une grande, est bien plus difficile à faire; ils partent de-là pour prouver qu'un Opéra-comique d'un Acte, réunissant plus de difficultés qu'une Comédie ou une Tragédie en cinq Actes, l'Auteur doit bien se garder de le traiter lestement.[9]

It does not seem rash to conclude from these various witnesses that in spite of the multiplicity and confusion of *genres* in the eighteenth century theater there was one constant interest, apparent in several *genres,* almost imperceptible at first, increasing in intensity as one advances in the century. Such decided attention to plot and the manner of its construction will inevitably be reflected in the comedy of the time. For example, Destouches wrote in 1745: ". . . à l'égard de *Molière,* on peut dire, sans lui faire injustice, que s'il est très-digne d'être imité, ce n'est pas par ses dénouemens, qui tiennent plus des Anciens et des farceurs d'Italie que des deux grands hommes que je nomme avec lui."[10] Voltaire's criticism of *le Misanthrope* has often been repeated. "L'auteur anglais a corrigé le seul défaut qui soit dans la pièce de Molière: ce défaut est le manque d'intrigue et d'intérêt; la pièce anglaise est intéressante, et l'intrigue en est ingénieuse; elle est trop hardie sans doute pour nos moeurs."[11]

Furthermore, the increasing importance given to plot as such was accompanied by a real interest in its mechanical construction; otherwise, comedy might have reverted to the incoherent state characteristic of the beginning of the seventeenth century. This was not likely to happen, however, in the presence of the incredible number of theoretical and, more particularly, practical treatises on the art of playwriting which appeared in the course of the century, especially in the second half. To be sure, the seventeenth century had already set the example with d'Aubignac's *Pratique du théâtre.* Whereas d'Aubignac seemed to have exhausted the possibility of the subject in a single volume devoted to all *genres,* Cailhava, by 1772, did not seem to regard four volumes as too many to

[9] *Théâtre,* 1781, v. 2, *le Nouveau marié,* Préface, p. 145.
[10] *Oeuvres,* 1757, v. 4, Seconde lettre à M. le Chevalier de B**, pp. 195–196. (Also in the 1745 edition.)
[11] *Oeuvres complètes,* 1879, v. 2, *Lettre sur la comédie,* 1734, p. 156, n. 3. Cf. also Prévost, *le Pour et le contre,* 1733, v. 1, pp. 80–96.

be given to a discussion of comedy alone. Indeed, by 1768 Charpentier complains thus:

> . . . la littérature est innondée de traités sur les principes. Il n'y a guère d'année où on ne publie une nouvelle poëtique. Vainement en reconnoït-on l'inutilité. Le préjugé qui a consacré les compilations de régles est plus fort. Il aveugle jusqu'à nos jeunes Auteurs. A peine ont-ils, par quelques essais, attiré les yeux du public sur eux, qu'ils s'érigent en Maîtres.[12]

In spite of this protest, however, Charpentier himself cannot resist the movement in which his contemporaries are losing themselves and he offers a feeble apology for adding another work to the already abundant collection:

> Il paroîtra singulier sans doute qu'après avoir dit que les régles sont pour les Arts qui exigent du génie, une cause infaillible de décadence, nous nous hazardions à en publier un Recueil. Nous ne nous y érigeons pas en législateur du Théatre. Nous considérons moins l'art en lui-même, que ses accompagnements. Nous ne donnons point les loix du Drame, mais les accessoires qui nuisent à ses progrès. Nous n'indiquons point les routes qu'il faut suivre, mais celles qu'il faut éviter.[13]

I do not propose to evaluate the work of Charpentier and others who wrote with a similar purpose;[14] the eighteenth century never arrived at a conclusive answer to this question. One may agree with dramatists like Piron[15] and Voltaire who decried the utility of any "rule" or one may agree with critics like Desfontaines[16] and Fréron[17] who were of the opinion that nature must be polished with

---

[12] *Causes de la décadence du goût sur le théâtre,* 1758, pp. viii–ix.
[13] *Ibid.,* p. xiii.
[14] Cf. in this connection Mornet, *la Question des règles au XVIIIe siècle* in R.H.L., 1914.
[15] *Oeuvres,* 1758, v. 1, p. xl. ". . . toutes les Poëtiques du monde (vinssent-elles des meilleures mains) ne furent ni ne seront jamais, je crois, non plus que nos Ouvrages d'agrément, que de Jolies inutilités?"
[16] *Observations sur les écrits modernes,* 1735, v. 3, pp. 313–314, *passim.* "Vous sçavez, Monsieur, que dans tous les Arts la théorie est nécessaire. . . . Je suis persuadé . . . avec M. de Voltaire que tous les raisonnemens sur l'Art Dramatique ne valent pas une Scène de génie, et qu'il y a bien plus à apprendre dans *Polieucte* et dans *Cinna,* que dans tous les préceptes de l'Abbé d'Aubignac. . . . Mais je n'en conclurois pas comme lui, *qu'il est inutile de parler de regles.*"
[17] *Lettres sur quelques écrits de ce tems,* 1749, v. 1, Lettre I, pp. 4–5. "Vous êtes persuadé, Monsieur, avec l'Auteur de *Zaïre,* que tous les raison-

art. Charpentier went so far as to say: "Les siécles qui servent d'époque à la décadence du goût, abondent en principes, et manquent de і.ons ouvrages."[18] Whether or not in the last analysis the first part of his observation is correct, the second is certainly applicable to the eighteenth century theater.

Nevertheless this passion for formulating codes is undeniably indicative of an *état d'esprit* which is concerned primarily with the form of things; as such, we accept it. It may be true, on the one hand, that this pedantic attention to form stifled genius; on the other, it was not without positive results for it served as a necessary check upon the ever-increasing tendency in eighteenth century comedy toward complexity of plot.

L'Ecole des femmes and *le Barbier de Séville* tell the same story, are based on the same general situation, deal with similar types of characters. As critics have pointed out the philosophical and moral significance of Molière, so have they lauded the technical superiority of Beaumarchais. The portrayal of character, the expression of moral truth was the chief preoccupation of Molière; an ingenious, perfectly constructed plot, that of Beaumarchais. It is true that each of these comedies is the expression of its author's peculiar genius. Is it not the part of genius to give concrete, lasting expression, also, to the theories and aspirations of an epoch? The comedy of Molière no longer satisfied the audience of Beaumarchais. Somewhere in the course of the century a new demand and a new set of values had arisen. It is this change in attitude, this shift in emphasis, which we wish to study.

nemens sur l'art dramatique ne valent pas une scéne de génie; et qu'il y a plus à profiter dans *Corneille* et dans *Moliere,* que dans *Aristote* et *d'Aubignac.* Mais en concluez-vous, comme lui, qu'il est *inutile de parler de régles?* Vous pensez que la théorie est nécessaire. C'est en vain qu'on a devant les yeux des chefs-d'oeuvres (*sic*), . . . si l'on n'étudie la nature, modéle de l'art.

"Les Ouvrages applaudis au Théâtre, ne donnent en les lisant qu'un goût de comparaison, et ne peuvent faire que des Copistes. C'est par de judicieuses remarques sur ces Ouvrages, et par l'application qu'on en fait aux loix du bon sens, qu'on peut parvenir à les égaler, et à juger des efforts de ceux qui s'exercent dans le même genre."

[18] *Op. cit.,* p. vi.

CHAPTER I

1700–1730

Indications at the end of the seventeenth century of an approaching change in opinion; Rapin, Hauteroche, Boursault.—Lesage and the preface to his *Théâtre espagnol* (1700).—J. B. Rousseau; Dufresny.—Complaints of lack of action in contemporary *comédie de moeurs* and *comédie de caractère;* Lafont's proposal to reduce the action of a five-act play to a single act.—Attacks against the episodic plays of Fuzelier and Pellegrin.

The period[1] intervening between Molière and Destouches is generally considered in dramatic history as a period of transition for it was not until 1730 and after, that the eighteenth century theater acquired that character termed "sentimental" which most sharply distinguishes it from the seventeenth century theater. This character was not acquired suddenly; it was the culmination rather of a series of gradual modifications the successive stages of which are visible in some of the comedies produced during these years of transition.[2] The movement which led during this period to a change in the tone of comedy was paralleled by a similarly slow expansion of the relatively narrow limits which had been assigned to the value of the plot of comedy and to its construction. We shall see how authors less gifted than Molière, after vainly striving to imitate him in painting contemporary manners and in creating living characters, are led by their own deficiencies and contemporary criticism of the *comédie de moeurs* and the *comédie de caractère* to center their attention on the plot of their comedies with the result that the plot as such begins to acquire a new value.

Although it is in a preface of Lesage that we find detailed refer-

---

[1] It should be stated that the chronological division into periods in no way represents the absolute cessation of one movement or phenomenon and the beginning of another; literary movements cannot be so sharply divided. It is for the sake of convenience and clarity that the whole has been divided into periods in which certain characteristics seem to be dominant but it should not be supposed that these traits will not recur intact or in a more fully developed form in the succeeding periods. The year 1775 has been taken as the *terminus ad quem;* we do not hesitate, however, to use the opinions of an author expressed after that date when they corroborate or complete his earlier views.

[2] Cf. Lanson, *Nivelle de La Chaussée et la comédie larmoyante,* 1887.

ences to what will be one of the main preoccupations of the century, there are also to be found in the writings of Rapin, Hauteroche and Boursault some indications in the latter part of the seventeenth century of the approaching change.

Long before Destouches and Voltaire expressed their criticisms of Molière,[3] the great seventeenth century dramatist had been severely taken to task by Père Rapin for the lack of care with which he arranged and ended his comedies: "Son Misanthrope est à mon sens le caractere le plus achevé, et le plus singulier, qui ait jamais paru sur le theatre. Mais l'ordonnance de ses Comedies est toûjours defectueuse en quelque chose, et ses denoüemens ne sont point heureux."[4] This simple, perhaps even inadvert, observation on the part of Rapin suggests that to him the disposition and *dénouement* of a comedy seemed more important than they had to Molière.

Hauteroche, one of the most popular of Molière's successors,[5] prefaced the majority of his comedies with words and ideas which will occur again and again in more elaborate form in eighteenth century writers. He tells us in the preface to *l'Amant qui ne flatte point* (1669) that were it not for the solicitation of his friends he would never have allowed his comedy to be played for ". . . il y avoit quelque Acte ou je ne voyois pas beaucoup de chaleur, et que l'action y languissoit, par la nécessité d'instruire le Spectateur de quelque circonstance."[6] The same desire to make the plot of his play more vivid and interesting led him to make *le Deuil* (1673) a one-act play.[7]

With remarkable frankness and with an appreciation of the demands of his "métier," Hauteroche points out the weakness of the plot and his manner of treating it in *le Feint polonois* (1686):

> Il y a deux actions qui n'ont gueres de rapport ensemble, et qui ne se mêlent presque point dans toute la Piece. On y voit la pluspart des Acteurs et des Actrices, agir suivant les intérêts qui les regardent en par-

[3] Cf. Introduction, p. 5.
[4] *Réflexions sur la poétique de ce temps,* 1675, p. 147.
[5] During the period 1700–1730 his plays were given on an average of twenty-seven times a year. (Cf. Joannidès, *la Comédie-Française de 1680 à 1900,* 1901.)
[6] *Oeuvres,* 1736, v. 1, p. 3.
[7] *Ibid.,* p. 429 (misprint for p. 427).

ticulier, sans se traverser l'un l'autre dans leurs desseins. . . . La Servante a peu de part dans l'intrigue, elle y agit selon que l'occasion se presente, sans avancer ni reculer les affaires de la Scene. Le dénouëment arrive par un incident imprévu que le hazard fait naître, mais qui pourtant ne choque point la vraisemblance.[8]

The preface to his last comedy, *les Bourgeois de qualité,* is evidence that by 1691 the desire for a comedy with some plot is in the air for critics have not failed to note in connection with his play that ". . . le sujet en est trop simple, et trop peu rempli d'incidens . . ."[9]

Almost simultaneously, in the preface to his *Esope à la ville* (1690), Boursault implies the existence of a similar criticism when he says:

> Cette comédie, à ce que disent les gens singuliers . . . n'a pas un assez grand noeud, ni assez de jeu de théâtre: et si cette piece a quelque mérite, c'est justement de là que je prétends le tirer. . . . avoir eu le secret de le (le noeud) faire assez petit pour ménager le terrain, et pour introduire sur la scene des personnages qu'on aime mieux y voir que les personnages du sujet même, c'est à mon sens ce qu'on en doit le plus estimer; ou, pour mieux dire, ce qu'on en doit blâmer le moins.[10]

Apparently, the fact that Boursault repeatedly interrupted the slight plot of his play to insert the moral tales of Aesop occasioned some criticism, very weak, however, as we shall see, in comparison with the storm of protest which greeted Pesselier in 1739 when he presented the public with an episodic play or *comédie à tiroirs.*

Nevertheless these remarks of Boursault are important in indicating a nascent interest in the plot of comedy as Hauteroche is important in being one of the first comic writers to give extended, concrete expression to his interest in his plots and their construction. The latter is interesting only as a forerunner and not as an initiator for with certain reserves,[11] he is content to follow in the

---

[8] *Ibid.,* v. 3, p. 339.
[9] *Ibid.* (preface bears no page numbers).
[10] *Oeuvres choisies,* 1811, v. 1, pp. 3-4.
[11] He says, for example, in the preface to his *Crispin musicien* (1680): ". . . je dirai en passant que nous avons quantité d'exemples de ces Personnages que ces Messieurs trouvent étrangers au Sujet, qui souvent ont fait naître au Théatre des plaisanteries fort spirituelles. Plaute et Terence n'ont point fait de difficulté de s'en servir; et l'illustre Moliere ayant suivi leurs

footsteps of his predecessors and his views, although indicative of new tendencies, are lacking in positiveness of expression and constructive suggestions. To Lesage belongs the honor of launching the manifesto and campaign of the century in the preface to his *Théâtre espagnol* published in 1700.[12]

Deliberately and not apologetically, Lesage sets out to improve the contemporary *comédie de moeurs*. His criticism of existing plays and his scheme for perfecting them are very original.

> . . . Tout le monde doit convenir que le Theatre François est parvenu pour la pureté des moeurs, à un point de perfection inconnuë aux autres Nations . . . Tous les differens caracteres du ridicule y sont peints avec des couleurs tres-vives et tres-réjoüissantes; et sur ce sujet il semble qu'il ait conservé une fecondité qui ne s'épuise point: mais il faut avoüer aussi qu'on y voit une secheresse d'intrigue étonnante; et je ne comprens pas pourquoy avec toute la délicatesse et tout le bon goût que nous avons, nos Auteurs, et les meilleurs mêmes, ont negligé ce qui sans contestation doit estre reputé l'ame et le principal fondement de toute l'action dramatique.
>
> Je ne craindray point d'avancer que les Espagnols en ont mieux jugé que nous, et qu'ils sont nos maîtres à imaginer et à bien conduire une intrigue. Ils sçavent exposer leur sujet avec un art infini, et dans le jour le plus avantageux. Ils joignent à cela des incidens si agréables, si surprenans, et ils le font avec tant de varieté, qu'ils paroissent aussi inépuisables sur cette matiere, que nos François le sont sur la diversité des caracteres ridicules. Ce n'est pas tout, les Pieces Espagnoles sont remplies de contre-temps ingenieux, de contrarietés dans les desseins des Acteurs, et de mille jeux de Theatre qui reveillent à tout moment l'attention du spectateur.[13]

traces, ne s'en est pas mal trouvé. Ce n'est pas que je veüille dire par là que ces exemples soient toujours bons à suivre; au contraire, je tiens que l'Art est un chemin bien plus certain, et que ses préceptes conduisent plus surement à la perfection, que ne font ces sortes de libertés, quoiqu'elles ayent été fort heureuses. Il est constant qu'on ne peut jamais déplaire avec l'Art, et qu'il est dangereux de s'écarter de ses regles; mais je crois qu'on n'est pas tout-à-fait condamnable, quand en le faisant on réussit, et qu'on trouve le moyen de plaire, qui est le but de ce grand Art." (*Op. cit.*, v. 2, pp. 6–7.)

[12] This is the only edition of the preface which accompanies his translation of Spanish plays. It has been republished by Cordier in his *Essai bibliographique sur les oeuvres d'Alain-René Lesage*, 1910, pp. 237–240. The importance of the preface was first pointed out by Lintilhac in his *Histoire générale du théâtre en France*, n.d., v. 4, *la Comédie, Dix-huitième siècle*, p. 156.

[13] *Théâtre espagnol*, 1700, Préface (no page numbers).

His express intention in publishing this volume of translations is to reveal to the public the pleasure to be derived from an ingenious plot and to encourage and stimulate his contemporaries to "s'attacher plus qu'ils ne font à l'intrigue de leurs Poëmes; par là ils rendront plus vif le plaisir que nous prenons aux spectacles."[14]

At the same time that he proposes to bring the *comédie de moeurs* to a higher degree of perfection by adding to it the qualities of a Spanish intrigue, and while he is suggesting to contemporary authors that they should give greater attention to the plots of their comedies, Lesage is not unaware of the obstacles confronting French dramatists. Spanish dramatists, unlike the French, are not required to observe the unities of time and place. Undaunted by such a formidable restriction, Lesage disposes of the problem in a simple, straightforward manner:

> Comme les Espagnols n'observent ny l'unité de lieu, ny la regle des vingt-quatre heures, et qu'à leurs figures outrées prés, il n'y a proprement que cela qui nous blesse dans leurs Comedies, j'ay gardé un milieu entre les libertés de leur Theatre, et la severité du nostre. Quand je ne puis, sans supprimer des incidens agreables, consommer l'action en un jour; je prens deux jours: mais cela ne va pas plus loin. Pour l'unité de lieu, il est impossible de la garder, sans oster le merveilleux, et sans tronquer les intrigues, qui sont, à mon sens, comme je l'ay déja dit, la plus ingenieuse et la plus noble partie de l'action dramatique.
>
> . . . pourvû que ces changemens (de lieu) soient bien ménagés, et que le spectateur en soit averti, je suis persuadé que c'est une fausse délicatesse de les trouver mauvais, et qu'en dépit d'Aristote et de nostre Tribunal dramatique, qui les condamnent, ils ne sçauroient nous rebuter.[15]

And so, with a determination and forcefulness which were rarely equaled in the eighteenth century, Lesage discards, whenever necessary, the unities of time and place. The majority of eighteenth century critics spent themselves in fruitless discussions of the verisimilitude or non-verisimilitude of the unities and their acceptance or non-acceptance by the ancients and the French classical dramatists. Lesage, spurred on by his intense interest in the plot of a play, rejects the unities because they restrict an exciting plot:

[14] *Ibid.*   [15] *Ibid.*

Je diray en finissant . . . que tant qu'un Auteur gardera l'unité de
lieu, il ne nous offrira que des intrigues tres-mediocres; et je crois qu'il
plaira moins au Parterre par le merite de cette servitude qu'il se sera
luy-même imposée, qu'il ne luy plairoit par la representation d'un grand
nombre d'incidens et de contre-temps agreables, que l'incommode et
gênante unité de lieu luy aura fait supprimer. Et par là il ostera toûjours à ses Poëmes plus de beautés, qu'il ne leur en pourra donner
d'ailleurs.[16]

Eight years later, in the *Critique de la comédie de Turcaret,*
Lesage suggests the same method for improving the contemporary
comédie de caractère:

Don Cléofas. . . . Mais dites-moi, seigneur Asmodée, quel bruit est-ce
que j'entends auprès de l'orchestre?
Asmodée. C'est un cavalier espagnol qui crie contre la sécheresse de
l'intrigue.
Don Cléofas. Cette remarque convient à un espagnol. Nous ne sommes
point accoutumés, comme les Français, à des pièces de caractère, lesquelles sont, pour la plupart, fort faibles de ce côté-là.
Asmodée. C'est en effet le défaut ordinaire de ces sortes de pièces:
elles ne sont point assez chargées d'évènemens. Les auteurs veulent toute
l'attention du spectateur pour le caractère qu'ils dépeignent; et je suis
de leur sentiment, pourvu que d'ailleurs, la pièce soit intéressante.[17]

The clause which terminates the end of this discussion is obviously
not in harmony with the theories Lesage has just been exposing
and to which he had already given expression. It seems logical to
conclude that he was pretending to make a concession, a mocking
concession which he in no wise believed himself.

During the first half of this period of transition the early effort
of Lesage to credit the plot of comedy with some importance is
practically unique. A less important observation or two on the part
of J. B. Rousseau and Dufresny, however, should not be ignored.

In the *Préface apologétique* to his *Capricieux* (1701) J. B.
Rousseau remarks that he had composed a fable relating to the subject-matter of his play which he would have inserted therein had
he not deemed it inappropriate to interrupt a dramatic action for
the sake of recounting a fable.[18] This conception is a distinct ad-

[16] *Ibid.*   [17] Second Dialogue.   [18] *Oeuvres,* 1712, v. 2, p. 341.

vance on that held by Boursault some ten years before. To a critic's objection that he has introduced into his play a young girl who leads his capricious hero around as she wills and by her dexterity forces him to act contrary to his wishes instead of as his capricious humour dictates, Rousseau replies thus:

> . . . mon but n'a pas été seulement de faire voir ce que c'est qu'un CAPRICIEUX; mais d'enseigner de quelle maniére il faut se conduire avec les gens d'une humeur capricieuse. Si la Comédie a quelque utilité, ce n'est pas tant de corriger les hommes, que de montrer ce qu'il faut faire pour vivre avec les hommes incorrigibles.[19]

Dufresny, in the prologue to his *Double veuvage* (1702), repeats practically verbatim the criticism which he had already expressed in the prologue to *le Chevalier joueur* (1697) of the contemporary author, and perhaps the contemporary audience, who seemed to consider sparkling wit the prime requisite of a comedy. The "marquis" and the "chevalier" argue thus:

> Le Marquis. Un homme sensé ne se rejoüit que des plaisanteries qui naissent du sujet.
> Le Chevalier. Que me fait le sujet à moi, il n'y a que cela qui m'ennuye.
> Le Marquis. Le sujet n'ennuye point, quand il est interessant. On aime à voir des caracteres soutenus, une intrigue nette et suivie, des situations qui surprennent, quoi qu'elles soient bien preparées, et de tems en tems quelque plaisanterie sans grossiereté.[20]

In 1715 Dufresny witnesses to a decided interest in the construction of a play and allows no excuse for the author who neglects what he considers the fundamental requisites of dramatic technique. The author should know "les regles de son art. Il seroit ridicule, par exemple, à un Architecte, de dire par modestie, qu'il ne sçait pas les regles de l'Architecture; ce seroit dire qu'il est un sot, car il doit sçavoir son métier."[21] He proposes to bring to light in a treatise on comedy[22] the pitfalls which beset the comic writer, but so far as we know, he did not carry out his intentions.

Toward the middle of this transitional period and thereafter until

[19] *Ibid.*, pp. 344–345.   [20] *Oeuvres*, 1731, v. 2.
[21] *Ibid.*, v. 4, *La Coquette de village*, Préface.
[22] *Ibid.*

the end we note a growing interest in the plot of comedy and scattered complaints by literary critics of the lack of action in the contemporary *comédie de moeurs* and the *comédie de caractère*.

For example, by 1713 Lafont is led to believe that without the genius of Molière an author cannot succeed in holding the attention of his spectators during the customary five acts of a comedy; he must obtain his effects by compressing the action of his play into a single act:

> . . . je suis d'avis que plus une action est serrée, et mieux elle fait son effet. Pourquoi les Comédies nouvelles en cinq Actes ont-elles tant de peine à réussir aujourd'hui, si ce n'est parce que le sujet en est souvent trop étendu? A moins que d'avoir le feu de Moliere, il est bien difficile de tenir pendant cinq Actes le spectateur en haleine. Il y a toujours beaucoup de vuide dans nos Comédies modernes, et j'aurois peut-être eu le malheur de ne pas réussir dans le même sujet, si je lui avois donné une plus longue étendue.[23]

Not only does Lafont propose to do away with the tediousness of contemporary comedy by centering his attention on the production of a rapid plot, but he goes a step further in the preface to *les Trois frères rivaux* (1713) when he states: "Un sujet, quand il est un peu traité, est seul capable de faire réussir une Piece . . ."[24]

Six years later Boindin expresses a similar point of view when he says, "Je doute que la simplicité soit un grand mérite dans un Poëme dramatique; plus on y agit, et plus on occupe le Spectateur."[25] Then, as if fearing the consequences of such a bold statement, he adds a qualifying clause to protect himself from the possible attacks of his more conservative contemporaries: "Je conviens toutefois qu'il ne faut pas porter la multiplicité d'incidens jusqu'à rendre une Piece confuse, il y a un juste milieu à prendre."[26]

This conciliatory attitude assumed by Boindin is adopted with more vigor and less hesitancy the following year in a criticism of the *Momus fabuliste* of Fuzelier.[27] Fuzelier undertakes to defend

---

[23] *Théâtre*, 1746, *l'Amour vengé*, Préface.
[24] *Ibid.*
[25] *Lettres historiques sur tous les spectacles de Paris*, 1719, p. 67.
[26] *Ibid.*
[27] ". . . quoique la piece aboutisse là (au mariage), elle est neanmoins sans dénouëment, et il ne peut même y en avoir, puisqu'il n'y a point de

mous critic for whom it is only "un assemblage grotesque de Scenes, sans liaison entre elles, où rien n'interesse, et où les personnages paroissent au hazard."[30]

Again, to judge from the evidence furnished by Pellegrin, the pure *comédie de caractère* is no more exempt than the episodic play from the demand for an interesting plot. As we have seen, Lesage suggested in 1708 the one acceptable means of repairing what was beginning to be considered a deficiency in the *comédie de caractère*. Unfortunately, however, the suggestion of Lesage seems not to have been successfully carried out for in 1726 Pellegrin found realistic grounds for the following imaginary conversation between Thalie and Momus:

> Thalie.
> . . . Messieurs les Inconstans, vous payerez pour tous,
> Je m'en vais lâcher contre vous
>
> Une piece de Caractere . . .   *
> Momus.
> De Caractere! Eh fy, personne n'y viendra.
> Venus.
> Personne!
> Thalie.
> Il est trop vrai, je l'avoüe à ma honte,
> Du beau, du vrai, du simple, on ne tient plus de compte,
> J'aurai fait de mon mieux, et ma piece ennuira,
> Melpomene ma soeur, en ces lieux me surmonte . . .[31]

These rebellious protests had acquired sufficient force by 1728 to occasion a counter-attack on the part of Buffier who points out that the merit of Molière's *Misanthrope* lies in the strongly marked characters rather than in the plot. He is also willing to grant that "l'intrigue des autres piéces de cet Auteur ne vaut guére mieux; et l'on convient assez univérsélement que ce n'est pas dans le noeu, ni dans le dénouement de ses piéces qu'il a réussi."[32] Does he conclude from this that his contemporaries should attempt to improve upon

---

[30] *Lettre de Mlle. de C** à Madame de N.** sur la comédie du "Nouveau Monde,"* 1722, p. 8.
[31] *Le Pastor-Fido,* 1726, Prologue, Scene III.
[32] *Suite de la grammaire française sur un plan nouveau ou Traité philosophique et pratique de poésie,* 1728, p. 94.

himself, not very successfully, against this critic who maintains that his comedy is unworthy of the name because of the poor disposition of the play. He weakly protests that, in spite of the tradition established by Boursault, his *Esope à la cour,* his *Esope à la ville* and similar comedies which demand a very light plot,

ce Docteur nouveau du Parnasse ne prêche que l'intrigue aux Auteurs Comiques, et il est difficile d'obéir à ses préceptes ; car comment imaginer ces changemens de noms, ces travestissemens de sexe, ces déguisemens de valets, et toutes ces merveilleuses situations qui font le prix d'une infinité de Comedies modernes.[28]

Fuzelier withstands with less assurance a severer attack than that experienced by Boursault some years before. Though consecrated by tradition, the *comédie à tiroirs* is being taken to task by more discerning critics for its lack of sustained plot.

Further proof of the increasing displeasure with which a comedy lacking in sustained plot was being regarded is to be found in Pellegrin's defense of his *Nouveau monde* (1723) :

Soit que l'action qui y est représentée se passe de Dieux à Dieux, de Dieux à hommes, où (*sic*) d'hommes à hommes, elle n'en est pas moins action, et par conséquent elle constitue une Comedie dans toutes les formes. . . . ces trois differentes especes d'actions, dont je viens de parler, aboutissent à la verité philosophique que j'ay établie cy-dessus, comme au centre d'unité. Que faut-il de plus pour honorer ce poëme du nom de Comedie ?[29]

But the beautiful philosophical truth which establishes the basic unity of the play is not sufficient to gain the approval of an anony-

---

noeud. Le commencement et la fin de la piece se répondent en quelque chose, puisque Venus épouse Vulcain, et que c'étoit ce que Jupiter s'étoit proposé; mais nous ne voyons point d'intrigue formée, pour ménager cet évenement et amener Venus au but que Jupiter se proposoit. . . . Il paroît donc que les parties de cette prétenduë Comedie n'ont nulle liaison entre elles, qu'elle est sans noeud et sans dénoüement, que l'évenement qui la termine dans la vingtiéme Scene, n'est point l'effet d'une intrigue qui l'ait préparé . . . que les Scenes qui la composent, sont pour la plûpart si independantes les unes des autres, qu'on pouroit les disposer au hazard, sans que la Piece en souffrit. . . ." (*Lettre Critique Ecrite à l'Auteur du Mercure, sur la Comedie qui a pour titre, Momus fabuliste, ou les Noces de Vulcain,* in *le Nouveau Mercure,* janvier 1720, pp. 91-94, *passim.*)

[28] *Momus fabuliste,* 1720, *Réponse à la Lettre Critique insérée dans le Mercure.*

[29] *Nouveau monde,* 1723, Préface.

Molière's conception of plot? On the contrary, since Molière's comedies were successful regardless of the presence or absence of plot, Buffier infers that plot is not as essential to comedy as some of his contemporaries seem to have imagined.

> Il ne faudroit donc peut-être pas se mettre si fort en peine de l'intrigue dans les Comédies: non pas qu'elle n'y puisse faire un agrément, quand elle est ingénieuse et naturéle . . . Mais afin de conserver la plus estimable prérogative de la Comédie, il vaut incomparablement mieux, en faire tomber le principal éfet sur la peinture des moeurs, et sur le vice dont il s'agit de faire sentir le ridicule et l'odieux. C'est l'éfet essentiel à la Comédie, au lieu que l'intrigue, du moins dans le goût d'aujourd'hui, n'est pas la partie la plus importante d'une belle Comédie.[33]

From a negative point of view these observations of Buffier are particularly significant as indicative of a reaction on his part against an existing interest in the plot of comedy; otherwise his protest would have no meaning.

Although the material describing the activity of this first or transitional period in the development of the values assigned to plot and its construction in comedy is less abundant than that which one finds later on—and this is quite natural since literary criticism was not in a flourishing state at the beginning of the eighteenth century —one can disentangle from the evidence here presented the beginnings of a new conception of the importance of plot. These are apparent in the early efforts of Lesage to infuse life into the *comédie de moeurs* and the *comédie de caractère* with the plot characteristic of the Spanish comedy; in the subsequent attempt of Lafont to vivify his play by concentrating the action, reducing the number of acts and discarding all foreign matter; in the timid declaration of Boindin that simplicity of action in a play may not be as great a beauty as hitherto imagined; in the protests which greet the episodic play, the *comédie à tiroirs,* of Fuzelier and Pellegrin; in the latter's plaintive assertion that a pure *comédie de caractère* no longer wins applause; and finally, in the warning of Buffier that his contemporaries are giving more attention than is necessary to the plot of their comedies. The observation of Buffier, however,

[33] *Ibid.,* p. 96.

strikes a discordant note and it is impossible not to feel that he is uttering a vain admonition.

The distinguishing characteristic of this period of transition is its spirit of protest and dissatisfaction with existing conditions. Although we have noted here and there an awakening interest in the plot of comedy, a new realization of its potential value, lack of concurrent opinion and concerted effort preclude the possibility of any marked advance in theory. It is to be expected, however, that the manifestations of discontent displayed during these early years of the century will eventually produce tangible results. The contemporaries of Lesage heedlessly ignored the solution he proposed for the problems confronting the eighteenth century theater. It was not until the second period of the development which we are tracing that authors began to realize its value.

CHAPTER II

1730–1750

Criticism elicited by the episodic comedy, the loosely constructed comedies of the Théâtre Italien and the *opéra-comique.*—Constructive suggestions by writers of regular comedy; Riccoboni; Destouches.—La Chaussée's exaggeration of the tendencies of Destouches.—The criticism of Collé.—Objections to the comedies of Marivaux.—A suggestion of Fréron.

At the very time that the *comédie larmoyante* reached the peak of success as a dramatic *genre,* the eighteenth century produced its two comedies which bear the greatest resemblance to established classical traditions: *la Métromanie* (1738) of Piron and *le Méchant* (1747) of Gresset. Because of the simultaneous success of these two distinct types of comedy, with adherence on the one hand to the traditional comic vein and dominance on the other of the newer and more serious tone, the history of comedy during this period presents a double aspect and an inevitable complexity. From our point of view, and in spite of its apparent complexity, a certain unity characterizes the comedy of this period. Whether the tone of comedy be serious or gay, real value is attached by authors and critics alike to the plot and its construction. According to eighteenth century critics, the effort made in this direction by certain authors is still insufficient and their failure calls forth adverse criticism almost without exception.

One of the most obvious indications of the increasing respect with which plot was regarded is the severe criticism elicited by the episodic comedy, by the loosely constructed comedies designed for the Théâtre Italien and by the *opéra-comique.*

As far as the first is concerned, Prévost and his contemporaries had decided that "le genre de ces sortes de Pieces décousuës, sans noeud et sans dénoüement, n'avoit pas un grand mérite, et parce qu'elles ressemblent plus à une Pasquinade qu'à une Comedie."[1] A few years later Desfontaines qualifies *les Deux nièces* as *spectacle*

---

[1] *Le Pour et le contre,* v. 2, 1733, p. 132.

since he refuses to honor with the name of comedy a play "où il n'y a ni plan, ni liaison, ni suite, ni intrigue, ni dénouëment, et qui ne consiste qu'en lieux communs, et en portraits, que font sans cesse des Personnages sans caractere et sans interêt."[2] *L'Ecole du temps,* an episodic play of Pesselier, aroused a bitter controversy[3] because of the refusal of some critics to call it a comedy on the ground that it lacked sustained plot. And the following year Pesselier provokes the unfavorable criticism of the author of *le Pour et le contre* because of the weakness of the allegory with which he attempted to link the scenes of his new play, *Esope au Parnasse.* Remembering the criticism which his *Ecole du temps* had aroused, he had decided that the unsuitable allegory which he had imagined was better than offering to the public "des Scénes absolument détachées, une Piece sans *Dénouëment* . . ."[4]

One of the critics of *l'Ecole du temps* attributed the weaknesses of the play to the fact that it had been written for the Théâtre Italien, "à qui les Scénes coupées et Episodiques conviennent . . ."[5] Since it was not unusual for authors who were unable or unwilling to satisfy the stricter requirements of the Comédie-Française to seek refuge in the freedom allowed by the Théâtre Italien, one would expect to find less regularity of plot structure in comedies designed for this theater. From this period on, however, the critic is rare who shows indulgence for these comedies when they lack sustained plot. The critic of Boissy's *Amours anonimes,* for example, attributes the success which the play enjoyed to the gay and lively tone in which it was written, but, he adds,

cela n'impose pas aux Gens qui ne cherchent dans les Piéces de Théatre, que ce qui est veritablement Théatral; ces Personnes . . . ont trouvé que dans les *Amours Anonimes,* il y avoit plus d'esprit qu'il n'en faut pour faire une Piéce d'un genre inferieur, c'est-à-dire une Piece (*sic*)

[2] *Observations sur les écrits modernes,* v. 7, 1737, p. 285.
[3] Cf. (a) *Mercure,* décembre 1738. (b) *Lettre d'un Provincial à son ami de Paris, au sujet de la Comédie de L'Ecole du Temps,* in 1739 edition of *l'Ecole du temps.* (c) *Lettre de l'Auteur de la Comédie de l'Ecole du Temps, à M. D. L. R. Auteur du Mercure de France. Pour servir de Réponse à une Lettre inserée dans le premier volume du mois de Decembre 1738, ibid.*
[4] *Réponse de M. Pesselier à la Lettre de l'Auteur du Pour et Contre, sur la Comédie d'Esope au Parnasse,* 1739, in *Oeuvres,* 1758, p. 51.
[5] *Lettre d'un Provincial à son ami de Paris, au sujet de la Comédie de l'Ecole du Temps, ibid.,* p. 54.

dont tout le tissu n'est qu'un assemblage de Scénes indépendantes les unes des autres; mais ils leur ont refusé le nom de Comédie, parce qu'il n'y avoit pas assés de fond pour mériter ce Titre, que bien de nos Modernes ne s'attachent gueres à remplir.[6]

About the same time Granet complains that the

Théatre Italien est depuis longtems en possession de donner des Pieces, où il n'y a ni intrigue, ni noeud, ni dénoument; on les nomme pourtant des Comédies. Seroit-ce à cause du ridicule qu'on y peint, et parce qu'elles sont déclamées par des Comédiens? On devroit plûtôt les appeler des Dialogues moraux et satyriques . . .[7]

In fact, critics are likely to show more indulgence for an author at the Théâtre Italien who has gone to the other extreme even when his play has not been successful. This happened in the case of *les Amans jaloux* whose author met with little success; nevertheless

les Connoisseurs ne laissent pas de lui rendre justice. On a trouvé sa Piéce bien écrite et bien conduite; il y a beaucoup plus d'action que dans bien d'autres qui n'ont dû leur reussite qu'aux beautés de détail . . . L'Auteur Anonime est peut-être tombé dans un autre excès; le noeud de sa Comédie a paru trop compliqué, pour pouvoir n'être mise qu'en trois Actes; la plupart des Scenes y paroissent écourtées; et l'action est si pressée qu'on diroit que la Scene est à Sparte, tant les interlocuteurs y sont laconiques; cependant à tout prendre ce dernier excès est infiniment plus pardonnable que le premier, qui fait dégenerer nos Comédies en conversations; nous avons souvent condamné ce défaut dans nos Journaux . . .[8]

By the end of the period it is not unusual to find similar criticisms directed against the *opéra-comique*. Whenever necessary, the *frères* Parfaict do not hesitate to condemn an *opéra-comique* which lacks at least a pretence of plot. They say of *le Bal du Parnasse* that this play "n'eut aucun succès, elle n'a ni intrigue ni liaison. Les Auteurs semblent n'avoir eu d'autre dessein que de placer sans

---

[6] *Mercure,* décembre 1735, v. 2, p. 2902. A criticism also repeated by Parfaict, *Dictionnaire des théâtres de Paris,* v. 1, 1756, pp. 119–120.
[7] *Réflexions sur les ouvrages de littérature,* v. 8, 1739, p. 111.
[8] *Mercure,* décembre 1735, pp. 2693–2694.

aucun art des traits critiques sur les ouvrages Dramatiques qui avoient paru sur les trois Théatres."[9]

Such criticisms as those which we have just cited did not, of course, prevent authors from writing episodic plays any more than the presence or lack of sustained plot invariably determined the success of an *opéra-comique* or a comedy written for the Théâtre Italien. They are extremely significant, however, in indicating the center toward which the thought of the period is converging.

It is in the criticism and conception of regular comedy, the *comédie de moeurs* and more especially the *comédie de caractère,* that we find the most authoritative assertions of the value of plot and the most decisive steps taken to secure for it universal admiration.

The complaints and suggestions of the preceding period continue. De Launay, for example, in 1733 expresses the fears which assailed him when he was composing *le Paresseux* because the inaction which must necessarily characterize his main character, Damon, might make the presentation of the play dull and lifeless. Since the simple portrayal of character no longer seems to be sufficient guarantee for the success of a *comédie de caractère,* he proposes to overcome the deficiency in his play by introducing Cidalise, a character who will compensate by her action for the languor of Damon.[10] In spite of his stated preferences for simple action, De Launay is compelled by external pressure to consider seriously the value of a complex plot for when the poet of the prologue warns the author not to deliver any tiresome sermons, the latter replies: "Je sçai qu'on est aujourd'hui pour l'intrigue. . . . Et même on ne hait point tant soit peu de Roman."[11]

It was not mere caprice that occasioned this increasing demand for plot, but the failure of authors to produce anything approaching in quality the *comédie de caractère* and the *comédie de moeurs* of Molière. We have seen that authors of the early years of the century were vaguely aware of their inability to produce forceful plays in either of these *genres*. As time goes on this consciousness

---

[9] *Dictionnaire des théâtres de Paris,* v. 1, 1756, pp. 362–363. (According to the preface, the work had been announced by 1750 so the manuscript of the early volumes had therefore probably been completed before that date.) Cf. similar criticisms, v. 2, p. 361; v. 3, p. 181.

[10] Préface.   [11] Prologue, Scene I.

increases, while the continued dearth of good plays provides excellent material for the field of contemporary criticism.

Up to this point the major part of the criticism which we have studied has been negative rather than positive, destructive rather than constructive. Nevertheless the slowly accumulating mass of concurrent opinion regarding the lack of action in contemporary comedy inevitably increased the weight necessary to shift the scale of values toward the side of plot. Under the existing pressure a partial change of emphasis was definitely accomplished with the simultaneous expression of the theories of Riccoboni and Destouches.

The conceptions of Riccoboni and his solutions to the problems confronting the contemporary writer of comedy are similar in spirit, if not wholly in detail, to those proffered some years earlier by Lesage; with the *Observations sur la comédie et sur le génie de Molière* we revert in several respects to the preface of the *Théâtre espagnol*. Whereas the publication of 1700 had had little immediate effect upon contemporary theory or criticism, the time was now ripe for suggestions which had earlier passed unnoticed and writers generally greeted the work of Riccoboni with enthusiastic approval.[12] We distinguish in the *Observations* three principal interpretations of the value of plot exemplified by (1) Riccoboni's dissatisfaction with and refusal to accept existing conditions, (2) his conception of the ideal *comédie d'intrigue*, and (3) immediate realization of this ideal being impossible, his conciliatory proposal of the indissoluble union of the *comédie d'intrigue* and the *comédie de caractère*.

Riccoboni's indictment of contemporary authors, although not particularly original, is important in that he attributes their failure

---

[12] (a) Merville, *les Mascarades amoureuses,* 1736, Préface, p. 4.
  (b) Desfontaines, *op. cit.,* v. 3, p. 314.
  (c) Mallet, *Principes sur la lecture des poètes,* 1745, p. 178.
  (d) Granet, *op. cit.,* v. 4, 1738, p. 65.
  (e) *Journal des Savants,* mars 1736.
  (f) *Lettres sur quelques écrits de ce tems,* 1749, v. 1, p. 5. The author reproduces an almost verbatim, but unacknowledged citation from the work of Riccoboni (p. 27). Fréron and La Porte collaborated in writing the *Lettres.* Since this same sentence occurs in the *Dictionnaire dramatique* of La Porte (1776, v. 1, p. 215), it is probably due to him.

not mainly to their inability to present living characters or to their superficial study of contemporary manners but to their lack of attention to plot. Spectators find themselves forced to prefer "des Comédies composées simplement de saillies et d'épigrammes, aux Comédies qui n'ont qu'une intrigue soutenue d'une diction simple et naturelle," and five-act plays whose action would scarcely suffice for a one-act play acquire an enviable reputation.[13]

Indeed, for Riccoboni, the plot and its construction constitute the essence of comedy. He very definitely states: "Comme l'*Intrigue* est la base du genre dramatique, c'est aussi la partie qui mérite une plus grande attention. Sans intrigue il n'y a point de Comédie . . ."[14] And elsewhere, "il est indubitable que, malgré l'opinion contraire de quelques Modernes, l'action et le noeud sont les objets les plus essentiels d'une Fable Dramatique."[15] He admits: "Les sujets, ou les Fables les plus simples, étoient autrefois les plus estimés, mais aujourd'hui qu'ils plairoient moins aux Spectateurs, on est obligé de les charger un peu, si on cherche à plaire en corrigeant les moeurs."[16]

If plot is the basis of comedy, a very essential part is the construction of this plot, which he defines as

la disposition naturelle et sensée du progrès de l'action, la façon de la faire marcher, l'ordre de toutes les parties, et principalement des Scénes, et la distribution convenable des incidens; enfin personne n'ignore que c'est par elle que le tout doit être disposé avec une telle harmonie, qu'il soit impossible, sans faire tomber l'édifice, d'en déranger la moindre partie, soit pour la changer de place, soit pour la retrancher.[17]

The whole work of Riccoboni is permeated with a boundless admiration for Molière who serves as a continuous illustration of all Riccoboni's cherished ideas. The high value which he attributes to plot and its construction, coupled with his enthusiasm for Molière, results in his finding in the plays of Molière consummate skill in this particular phase of dramatic art. He believes that "Moliere nous a fait sentir dans ses meilleures Piéces l'extrême attention qu'il a eue à faire marcher l'oeconomie du tout ensemble avec celle

---

[13] *Observations sur la comédie et sur le génie de Molière*, 1736, p. 67.
[14] *Ibid.*, p. 4.
[15] *Ibid.*, pp. 216–217.
[16] *Ibid.*, pp. 45–46.
[17] *Ibid.*, pp. 49–50.

des parties de la Fable, et de quelle conséquence il a regardé ces deux objets pour la perfection du Poëme Dramatique."[18] He does not agree with those critics who are of the opinion that "les dénoumens de Moliere, bien loin d'être parfaits, sont très-défectueux. Cette décision me paroît d'autant plus injuste, que Moliere, à mon avis, est supérieur dans cette partie à ceux qui l'ont précédé, et peut-être à ceux qui l'ont suivi."[19] And he spends no little time lauding the perfection of Molière's plots, the superiority with which he arranges his actions and the excellent manner in which he brings them to a conclusion.

Whether or not Riccoboni's judgment of Molière is correct is of little import to our discussion. Buffier was probably more correct when he said in 1728: ". . . l'on convient assez universélement que ce n'est pas dans le noeu, ni dans le dénouement de ses pièces qu'il a réussi."[20] It is characteristic of eighteenth century writers to impute to Molière whatever for the moment they considered the essential part of a play. Even justification of the *comédie larmoyante* on these grounds was not uncommon.[21] That Riccoboni should insist upon the superiority óf Molière in the plot, its construction and its *dénouement* is important from our point of view in that it is incontrovertible evidence of the high place which they occupied in his scale of values and indicative of the extent to which the comedy of the eighteenth century was unconsciously deviating from the ideals of Molière.

Further proof of Riccoboni's confidence in the value of plot is found in his interesting project for reforming the contemporary theater by means of a new *comédie d'intrigue*. Riccoboni distinguishes two kinds of plot.[22] In the first, none of the characters plans to thwart the action; it apparently proceeds on its course of its own accord only to be interrupted by events seemingly due to pure chance. This kind of plot, he believes, is the most perfect and produces the greatest effect, for the spectator will much prefer attributing the obstacles which arise to the caprices of fortune rather than to the malignity of an old master or his valet. A comedy based

18 *Ibid.*, pp. 51–52.   19 *Ibid.*, p. 123.
20 Cf. Chapter I, p. 17, n. 32.
21 Cf., for example, Du Perron de Castera, *Lettre à Monsieur Louis Riccoboni*, 1737, p. 19.
22 For the two following paragraphs cf. *Observations*, pp. 5 f.

on a plot of this nature is a much more faithful representation of daily events and is therefore more "vraisemblable." The *Amphitryon* and the *Menaechmi* are the only two examples of the ancients' interest in this type of plot the perfection of which Plautus blunted by introducing a supernatural element. Spanish writers have frequently employed this kind of plot—*la Maison à deux portes* of Calderon is a model in the *genre*—but have usually spoiled it because of the extreme licence admitted on their stage.

If in the first kind of plot it is chance which produces all the incidents, in the second, which is more common and less difficult to construct, nothing happens which has not been premeditated. We have either a son in love with the person whom his father wishes to marry and who imagines a ruse to attain his end or a young girl who, about to be married to someone she does not love, inspires a lover, a "soubrette" or a "valet" to dissuade her parents from the proposed alliance. In this case, all the events are the result of pure design on the part of the characters and the spectator's pleasure in the play is lessened by the fact that he is often able to foresee the occurrence of these incidents before they actually take place.

To be sure, this second kind of plot is easier to create than the first and yet, says Riccoboni,

> on ne peut assez admirer que les modernes ne se soient point exercé sur des sujets, et n'aïent point inventé des plans, où les incidens fussent produits, amenés par le hazard, ou les seules circonstances. . . .
> Il faudroit donc, pour composer une excellente Comédie, s'attacher uniquement à la premiere espéce, et ne rien emprunter de la seconde. Le Théatre, si on l'ose dire, commence à vieillir; les nouveautés seules peuvent lui redonner de la vigueur. Mais loin de la chercher dans les détails d'un dialogue singulier ou satirique, ou dans des caractéres outrés, et hors de la nature, il faudroit la tirer, cette vigueur, du sein même de la fable ou du sujet; alors le fonds des Piéces auroit moins d'uniformité, et les situations plus variées par conséquent, deviendroient aussi plus neuves et plus interessantes, sans rien perdre de leur vraisemblance.[23]

Riccoboni's proposal of a *comédie d'intrigue* where the main interest lies in events which are determined by a chance combination of circumstances is as original as it is curious; his play will be ex-

[23] *Ibid.*, pp. 12–14.

purgated of the supernatural element of ancient comedy and the extravagances of Spanish comedy. We must not overlook the fact that he hastens to add at the end of his discussion: "Mais à quelque genre d'intrigue que l'on s'attache, on doit toûjours s'accommoder aux moeurs des tems et des lieux. . . . par *moeurs,* j'entends avec les Anciens ce que l'on appelle aujourd'hui *caractéres* . . ."; [24] he shows thereby that the pendulum had not yet swung far enough to permit an assertion like Diderot's "c'est aux situations à décider des caractères." No, the day was not yet at hand for the acceptance of a comedy the sole interest of which lay in a clever combination of events and circumstances. It was necessary to wait until the time of Beaumarchais for the realization of an analogous, if not identical, conception. From the point of view of the characters in the play, what, if not a chance combination of circumstances, determines the main incidents of *le Barbier de Séville?* In reply to Suzanne's comment, "Aucune des choses que tu avais disposées, que nous attendions, mon ami, n'est pourtant arrivée!", Figaro of *le Mariage* describes perfectly the technique which Beaumarchais had employed in *le Barbier:* "Le hasard a mieux fait que nous tous, ma petite. Ainsi va le monde; on travaille, on projette, on arrange d'un côté; la fortune accomplit de l'autre . . . tous sont le jouet de ses caprices . . ." [25]

It is not necessarily true that Beaumarchais was indebted to Riccoboni for his conception of a *comédie d'intrigue* where the main interest lay in the ingenious combination of several circumstances. Forty years of mutations and variations in the importance given to plot intervened between the expression of Riccoboni's idea and Beaumarchais' realization of a similar one, forty years of theory which needed the stamp of Diderot to clear the way for Beaumarchais and to complete the latter's own theories. Yet it is not impossible to suppose that Beaumarchais was acquainted with the work of Riccoboni. As we have tried to show, he was well known as a dramatist; his *Observations* met with immediate success and were cited with respect. As late as 1760, in the *Eloge historique de M. Fagan* which appeared in the first volume of Fagan's works, the author adopts and paraphrases Riccoboni's original

[24] *Ibid.,* pp. 14–16, *passim.*   [25] IV, 1.

idea without acknowledging the source.[26] At any rate, whether or not the author of *le Barbier* was acquainted with the author of the *Observations,* to Riccoboni belongs the honor of having been the first to express a formula which Beaumarchais has the greater honor of having successfully put into practice.

We have seen Riccoboni's dissatisfaction with existing conditions and his proposal for their improvement. No one was more conscious than he, however, that the immediate realization of his ideal was impossible. In spite of his evident predilection for the plot of comedy, as proved by his eulogy of Molière and his suggestion for a new kind of *comédie d'intrigue,* he concludes by centering his attention elsewhere, by adopting an attitude of conciliation compatible with the period, an attitude which was rich in evolutionary force and a definite step forward in the development which we are tracing; he culls and completes the earlier suggestion of Lesage.

Lesage had suggested that his contemporaries might improve their *comédies de caractère* by adding to them the plot characteristic of Spanish comedy. Riccoboni goes a step further and proclaims that a *comédie de caractère* without plot is a monstrosity and should not be tolerated. He apparently renounces his former revolutionary idea and returns to orthodox observations before assuming his final, conciliatory attitude. He states that

> Les Piéces de caractére sont plus goûtées aujourd'hui que les Piéces d'intrigue, non-seulement parce que les premieres ont sur les secondes l'avantage de la nouveauté, mais encore parce que celles-ci ne sont que l'ombre de la vérité, et que les autres en sont une image fidelle.

He adds, however, that many French authors have claimed that

> une Comédie de caractére n'étoit pas susceptible d'intrigue, ou qu'elle ne l'étoit que d'une intrigue très-légere; que le caractére une fois trouvé, c'étoit le point essentiel auquel un Poëte devoit s'arrêter, qu'il n'y avoit

[26] P. xxxi. "Cette Comédie est du meilleur genre des Pieces d'*intrigue;* celles qui sont produites par le hazard et par le concours naturel des circonstances, étant préférables de beaucoup à celles que les personnages . . . imaginent et conduisent. Dans celles-ci, c'est à proprement parler le spectateur seul que l'on embarrasse: dans les autres, les Acteurs eux-mêmes se trouvent embarrassés, et ce doit être nécessairement la source d'un plaisir de plus."

point d'autre moïen d'attacher le Spectateur, et que ni l'un ni l'autre ne
devoient s'embarasser si la Fable est intriguée, ou ne l'est pas.

Pour moi je regarde une Comédie de caractére sans intrigue, comme
un corps sans ame . . .

Le caractére doit lui-même servir à intriguer l'action, et c'est de cette
source que l'intrigue doit partir.[27]

And so, what Lesage had dared propose as a means of improvement, as a possible addition to the *comédie de caractère,* becomes
with Riccoboni an essential and integral part of the play, "l'âme
du corps," as he calls it. He reconciles what had been two distinct
conceptions by *raising the plot of comedy to the plane occupied by
its characters.*

If this were an isolated example of a shift in emphasis, it might
be passed over lightly. It was fortified and intensified, however, by
the simultaneous expression of a similar opinion on the part of
Philippe Néricault Destouches, one of the eighteenth century's
most popular and admired dramatists.

Destouches expressed the same intentions as Dufresny some
years before of presenting to the public in finished form what his
reflections and experiences as a dramatist had taught him about
dramatic art, but no more than Dufresny did he carry out his intentions.[28] From the prefaces and notices which precede the majority of his plays, however, one can obtain a fairly clear idea of
the relatively high place occupied by the plot and its construction
in the dramatic theories of Destouches.

We must begin by acknowledging that Destouches' predilection
for the *comédie de caractère* is evident from a mere enumeration of
his plays since approximately half of them bear titles indicating
that character-study is the main concern of the play: *l'Irrésolu,*
for example, *l'Ambitieux, le Glorieux, le Dissipateur, l'Ingrat,* etc.
Furthermore, critics have generally agreed that, apart from isolated attempts at *comédie de caractère,* such as those of Gresset and
Piron, Destouches exhibited the most persistent efforts to rehabilitate the *genre* in the first half of the century. His interest in the

[27] *Op. cit.,* pp. 27–30, *passim.*
[28] *Suite de la lettre III à Monsieur le Chevalier de B**,* in *Oeuvres,* 1758,
v. 7.

comédie de caractère is particularly fortunate from our point of view for in comparing his conception and treatment of *comédie de caractère* with those generally accepted as classical we can determine the extent to which classical views were being modified.

One of the most significant of Destouches' theories is that an author who proposes to portray a character on the stage not only must portray him as fully as possible but must place him "au milieu des circonstances où il produit le plus d'effets intéressans."[29] He admits that his difficulty does not consist in finding a character suited to representation on the stage; "la véritable difficulté consiste à le placer dans un personnage convenable, et à l'environner des circonstances qui peuvent servir à le mieux développer."[30] These statements of Destouches are not merely of passing interest —they touch upon exceedingly important principles. With the best of intentions and probably in spite of himself Destouches is shifting his attention from the psychological interest afforded by the study of character to the external circumstances of the play, to the events through which his hero will move. If he cannot portray characters strong enough in themselves to determine the events of the play, he is forced to resort to external circumstances to put them in motion. Destouches has admitted that, after determining the nature of his characters, his main concern is to place them in situations which will have the most potent effect on their development. Consequently, we shall not be surprised to hear Diderot proclaim a few years later that it is these very situations which must determine the characters.

The interest that Destouches shows in the plot with which he will surround his hero rather than in the hero himself is probably the result of sheer inability to achieve anything better. On the other hand, he is no less aware than De Launay that a play devoted exclusively to the psychological study of character is likely to meet with indifference and we find him reiterating authoritatively a refrain analogous to that of Riccoboni, namely, that a comedy composed "et d'intrigue et de caractére . . . est le plus sûr moyen de plaire."[31]

---

[29] *L'Ambitieux*, 1737, Préface.   [30] *Ibid.*
[31] *La Fausse Agnès* (1736), Prologue (written according to Hankiss, *Destouches*, p. 135, before 1727).

While plot should share alike with character in arousing and sustaining the interest of an audience, it is by attention to the former that Destouches hopes to achieve the latter. He tells us, for example, in the preface to *l'Irrésolu* that, had it not been for the possible superficiality and *invraisemblance* caused by the restricting unity of time, his first intention had been to "mettre en oeuvre un grand nombre d'incidens propres à caractériser (son)· héros." Instead, he felt forced to limit himself to the incidents which constituted the framework of the plot and, as he himself says, "Pour annoncer mon *Irrésolu,* je me contentai de bien faire son portrait, par le récit de diverses circonstances qui avoient précédé l'action . . . Et je me repentis (après la représentation) de n'avoir pas mis en action, quelques-unes des circonstances qui n'étoient qu'en récit." A similar difficulty confronted Destouches in writing *le Dissipateur,*[32] because it is manifestly impossible, according to him, for a spendthrift, no matter how extravagant he may be, to come to total ruin in the time allowed by the classical unities. There was no alternative except to present his hero on the brink of ruin, knowledge of which had been withheld from him by his own blindness and false friends. But "il falloit faire connoître au Spectateur les raisons et les incidens qui l'avoient causée; je ne pouvois les mettre en action, puisque le temps ne me le permettoit pas, et ce n'est que par des récits que j'ai rempli mon sujet . . ." And Destouches considers this a weakness for which he feels obliged to apologize.

The important rôle played by the *intrigue romanesque* in the comedies of Destouches has already been noted by critics of the *comédie larmoyante* as well as by biographers of Destouches. In this connection Destouches' acknowledged admiration for the repertoire of Thomas Corneille has also been pointed out.[33] It is unfair to Destouches, however, to overlook the fact that he delights not only in the ingenuity and inventiveness which Corneille displays in choosing his subjects, but also in his "disposition des sujets. Jamais homme . . . n'a mieux possédé l'art de bien conduire une Pièce de théatre . . ."[34] Whatever *romanesque* element there may be in his comedies, it is evident from his prefaces that Destouches attempted to control it by studied technique and atten-

---

[32] Préface, in *Oeuvres,* 1745, v. 6, pp. 482–483.
[33] Cf. Hankiss, *op. cit.,* p. 266.   [34] *Oeuvres,* 1757, v. 4, p. 196.

tion to play-construction; it was his desire to remain in the domain of the probable.

In the general preface to the 1745 edition of his plays we find an excellent example of this. He says, ". . . j'ai ajoûté, retranché, ou refondu des Scénes entieres; j'ai porté même la correction jusqu'à faire des Actes nouveaux, principalement des Actes cinquiémes, ordinaire écueil des Auteurs Dramatiques . . ."[35] A logical, even plausible, *dénouement* was the least of Molière's concerns—for Destouches it becomes of prime importance. He laments the fact that many excellent, even brilliant plays fail to obtain success because of a weak last act and he explains such failure thus:

> C'est que pour se livrer trop tôt à leur feu, ils ont négligé l'article le plus essentiel. La contexture de leur fable est-elle mal construite, ou confiée au hasard? Le dénoûment n'en peut être heureux, quoiqu'elle puisse produire de très-grandes beautés. Mais où nous conduisent-ils, ces écarts brillans? A la plus honteuse catastrophe . . . Toutes parties qui n'ont pas cet assortiment, d'où résulte un tout bien symétrisé, ne peuvent aboutir à la même fin; cependant c'est cet heureux accord des parties, ce sont leurs justes proportions, qu'il faut toujours regarder comme le plus sûr et l'unique moyen d'y parvenir: chef-d'oeuvre d'un génie qui se posséde, et qui se laisse guider par l'art et par la raison.[36]

This explanation of the failure which awaited many plays is at once indicative of the premium Destouches set upon the construction of his plot and of the whole tendency of the eighteenth century, in default of *fond,* to seek quality and beauty in the way in which an idea is presented rather than in the idea itself. This attention to form is significant not only of Destouches' lack of genius,[37] but of the general dramatic incompetency of the whole century. At this early stage in the history of eighteenth century comedy we have definite evidence of the tendency, which later becomes the rule, of checking genius and spontaneity for the sake of studied technique, careful composition, a logical *dénouement.* This is the first expression of an idea which will gain footing and be carried to the inevitable extreme with Diderot. In other words, we enter definitely upon the path which will terminate in the demand for a

[35] P. v.   [36] *Ibid.,* pp. vi–vii.
[37] Cf. Hankiss, *op. cit.,* pp. 393–394.

"pièce bien faite"; when an author has nothing to say, he is compelled to center his attention upon how he will say it.

Destouches, however, marks not the end, but the beginning of an evolution. We have seen how he raises the value of plot to the level occupied by character; how he centers his attention on the action as a means of attaining the latter; how zealously he works to produce a play which will be "bien faite." Nevertheless, although Destouches opens the way to Diderot, he is not Diderot and so we often find his own, newer ideas interfused with good classical tradition. Side by side with his admonition that the author should search for situations adapted to developing his character, we find him attempting to establish an intimate union between the action and characters of *l'Ambitieux et l'Indiscrette*. Having found the character who will provide the comic element of the play, he says:

> . . . je m'attachai avec soin à le rendre essentiellement nécessaire; je fis sortir de son caractere les principaux événemens de la piéce. Et c'est en effet de ces indiscrétions qui font naître les incidens qui forment le noeud et qui accélerent le dénouement. Je le liai si intimement à la construction de tout l'ouvrage qu'il en est inséparable . . .[38]

Although we have seen above that the desire to surround his characters with favorable events was one of the principal preoccupations of Destouches, this last citation shows that the idea did not dominate him to the exclusion of all others—the pendulum has not yet swung that far.

No, Destouches still has faith in the indissoluble union which should exist between the characters and the action of his play. In spite of his contribution to accelerating the eighteenth century's growing tendency to shift the emphasis to the latter, he would rather believe in the importance of the former; he is not wholly willing to sacrifice character to action and yet he is forced to admit in the preface to his *Dissipateur* that in order to enliven the play and to make it interesting,

> je n'ai pû me dispenser de mettre en oeuvre tous les caracteres épisodiques, qu'il amenoit nécessairement à sa suite, et qu'il ne m'a pas été possible de me renfermer dans un petit nombre de Personnages et d'événe-

[38] *Oeuvres*, 1745, v. 7, pp. 10–11.

mens, ni d'affecter cette admirable simplicité d'action, si justement admirée dans les Anciens . . .[39]

And we find him contemplating with a feeling akin to envy the miraculous situations, "la magie perpétuelle," which the liberty of the English stage allowed Shakespeare in the *Tempest:* "Et quels incidens ne peut-on point amener par la force de la magie? que nous serions heureux en ce pays-ci, . . . si on vouloit nous permettre de nous servir d'un art si commode! que de belles choses ne ferions-nous point!"[40]

With the simultaneous expression, then, by two distinguished contemporaries of the same general principle, a definite step forward was taken in the development which we are tracing; the position assumed by the one was fortified by the principles expressed by the other. Both Riccoboni and Destouches cling tenaciously to the *comédie de caractère* as the ideal type of play and yet by their concerted effort the plot of comedy is raised to the important position occupied by character. Destouches did not give concrete expression to his conception until 1736, date of the publication of *la Fausse Agnès*. His contemporaries were earlier aware of his intentions and although they did not always approve of them or even consider that he had carried them out, they did not fail to remark the change in values toward which he was tending. An anonymous critic of *le Philosophe marié,* for example, wrote in 1727: ". . . je trouve que cette Comédie n'est ni une Piece d'intrigue, ni une Piece de caractere, quoyqu'il me paroisse que le dessein de l'Auteur estoit qu'elle fût l'une et l'autre tout ensemble."[41]

Once the initial step has been taken in modifying the value previously assigned to the plot of comedy, once plot is raised to the high level formerly occupied by character, the stage is set for the rôle which it occupies in the plays of La Chaussée. Indeed, it is impossible to understand the value which La Chaussée accredited to plot without having first understood the value assigned to it by his predecessor. For Destouches, action, plot and its perfect con-

---

[39] *Oeuvres,* 1745, v. 6, pp. 483–484.
[40] *Oeuvres,* 1757, v. 4, p. 212. For the influence of the English theater on Destouches, cf. Hankiss, *op. cit.,* pp. 32–36; 270–274.
[41] *Relation curieuse de tout ce qui s'est passé au Parnasse au sujet des Comédies du Philosophe marié et de l'Envieux,* 1727, p. 7.

struction serve as a means to an end. Under the impetus given by
Destouches, it will be easy for La Chaussée to go one step further
and allow the means to become the end.

In his admirable study of Nivelle de La Chaussée M. Lanson
has shown that for the innovator of the *comédie larmoyante*
comedy itself is little other than an *intrigue romanesque,* intention-
ally complex and based upon an initial false situation.[42] M. Lanson
attributes the predominance of an *intrigue romanesque* to the peculiar nature of *sensibilité,* for the characters of a play as conceived by La Chaussée are so simple, so naïve themselves that the
play could not subsist without complexity of plot. Since his characters, in virtue of their innate goodness, cannot be kept apart except through a misunderstanding, there would be no play if endless
incidents and multiple complications did not prevent them from
immediately divining the *dénouement.*[43] M. Lanson has said that
La Chaussée's conception of plot complication is not the result of
poor disposition of subject-matter, or simple lack of skill on the
part of the author, but "un arrangement réfléchi, voulu, un art ou
tout au moins un artifice raisonné" the technique of which consists
in piling up the action in the beginning of the play and keeping the
spectator - in suspense by mysteriously postponing the exposition
until the end.[44]

It is undeniably true that *sensibilité,* taken in the sense of the desire to portray "des âmes sensibles," increased the importance
which La Chaussée assigned to the plot of his plays and helped to
precipitate a movement already in progress. It does not seem wise,
however, to consider *sensibilité* the sole factor influencing La
Chaussée's conception and construction of plot for, as we shall see
later, the fact that Diderot wished as much, if not more, than La
Chaussée to portray "des âmes sensibles" did not prevent him from
forming a slightly different conception of the value of plot and a
totally different conception of its construction. If *sensibilité* in itself invariably produced a fixed type of plot, an inflexible conception of its construction, we could not account for the different
ideas prevalent in the second half of the century. When, during the

---

[42] *Nivelle de La Chaussée et la comédie larmoyante,* pp. 173–187, *passim.*
[43] *Ibid.,* pp. 240–241.   [44] *Ibid.,* pp. 177–178.

period which we are studying, *sensibilité* invaded the theater, it found fertile soil in the field of comedy for it was the prevailing, if not absolutely universal, opinion that the potential values which lay dormant in the plot of comedy had been neglected and should be cultivated. Considered in the light of the increasing importance with which complexity of plot was being viewed, it is not surprising that La Chaussée resorted to the *intrigue romanesque.* Should one not see, therefore, in the success of the *comédie larmoyante* the coalescence of two distinct tendencies, independent of each other yet peculiarly adapted to reciprocal influence? Should the occasion arise, and the occasion did arise, for a different conception of the importance of plot-construction, the quality which is *sensibilité,* whatever its contribution to modifying the accepted conceptions of the value of plot, would be impotent to prevent those conceptions from proceeding along their natural course of development.

To attribute the success of the *comédie larmoyante* solely to the vogue of *sensibilité* or to the growing interest in plot as such or even to a combination of both factors would be equally false. The new successes of the novel, especially the English novel, were most probably a third factor in influencing its growth. It was natural to transmit to the stage some of the characteristics of a relatively new and successful *genre* and contemporary writers did not hesitate to do so. M. Mornet has called attention, for example, to the existence of an *Elixir du sentiment* (1755) which is nothing other than a *mise en roman* of *Cénie,* a *comédie larmoyante* of Mme. de Grafigny, proving that the play was a novel in dialogue rather than a dramatic production.[45] It is not within the aim of this investigation to evaluate the foreign influences which aided in determining the nature of the eighteenth century French theater. One should indicate in passing, however, that the causes for the popularity of the *comédie larmoyante* with its *intrigue romanesque* are complex and the result of several factors, that it is not wise to insist too much upon any one of them because it was not one circumstance, but a combination of circumstances which determined its vogue.

Whatever the causes for its success, there is no doubt about the fact of that success, and a complicated, romanesque plot becomes an ideal of writers during the second decade of this period. As

[45] R.H.L., 1915, pp. 610–611 (review of G. Noël's *Madame de Grafigny*).

M. Lanson has pointed out, there are certain vices inherent in the *genre* as conceived by La Chaussée; La Chaussée defeats his own ends by supposing so much action that the greater part of it must be entrusted to long narrations. As a result, the action of the play, especially the first part, is exceedingly slow and tedious. Contemporary critics were quick in perceiving these vices and along with endless discussions about the violation of classical rules and the inadvisability from a moral point of view of uniting the serious and the comic there are some pertinent attacks against the faulty construction of the *intrigue romanesque*. Practically all critics unite in proclaiming that it does not allow sufficient action to take place on the stage.[46] The most complete and penetrating criticism of the *intrigue romanesque* was made at the end of the period by Collé.

It is surprising and gratifying to see how ably Collé indicated the defects of the plot of the *comédie larmoyante* in his criticism of Mme. de Grafigny's *Cénie*. According to our critic, the weaknesses of *Cénie* result not only

de la construction de la pièce; mais encore plus de la foiblesse et du vice du genre *larmoyant*. Dans cette espèce de drame, un auteur n'a jamais et ne peut pas même avoir assez de temps pour exposer nettement son sujet, et pour faire toutes les préparations nécessaires à l'intelligence de sa pièce. . . .

Un autre défaut, qui est encore inhérent à ce genre, c'est l'obligation de cacher le dénouement, et d'empêcher qu'on ne le devine; ce qui est cause, presque toujours, que l'exposition dure jusque dans les derniers actes, et que l'on a encore des faits, même au cinquième acte, dont il faut instruire le spectateur; et rien au monde n'est plus froid que le récit de ces faits, qui coupe presque toujours indispensablement l'action, et justement dans le temps où tout est davantage en mouvement, et où cela dérange nécessairement les situations les plus vives et dans lesquelles il doit y avoir le plus de chaleur . . . aussi la plupart du temps, dans les derniers actes de ces pièces, les personnages s'entendent-ils à demi-mot, et le plus souvent encore se devinent-ils. Quelquefois même, comme l'auteur sait que les spectateurs sont au fait, il les fait dispenser bravement de

---

[46] For example (a) Prévost, *le Pour et le contre*, v. 5, 1734, pp. 362–363.
    (b) Desfontaines, *Observations sur les écrits modernes*, v. 1, 1735, p. 29.
    (c) Contant d'Orville, *Lettre critique sur la comédie intitulée l'Enfant Prodigue ou l'Ecole de la Jeunesse*, 1737, p. 26.

s'éclaircir absolument entr'eux; enfin, le plus grand vice de ce genre,
. . . c'est le manque total de vraisemblance.[47]

Collé agrees with modern critics that in the plays of La Chaussée
there is "un peu plus d'entente et de connoissance du théâtre, des
scènes mieux liées et mieux enchaînées; les préparations sont plus
adroitement faites, et l'on y voit plus en général, ce qu'on appelle
la main de l'artiste."[48]

Collé, then, bases his condemnation of the *comédie larmoyante*
on the weak technique and poor construction of its plot. Not only
does the dramatist suppose so many events to motivate his action
that there is not time enough to expose them in the beginning of the
play, but he is forced thereby to extend his exposition to the last
act and interrupt the logical course of the plot at strategic points to
insert a recital of anterior events. Nor does Collé fail to point out
the flaw in the plot-technique of the *comédie larmoyante* which was
most instrumental in causing a reaction against the *intrigue romanesque*. This flaw was the postponement and concealment from
the spectator not only of the outcome of the plot but of the events
and clues leading up to it. The poor results obtained by writers of
comédie larmoyante, their exploitation instead of their domination
of the vices inherent in the *genre* eventually led to a re-evaluation
of the *intrigue romanesque* and to a desire for something different.

While the value assigned to the plot by Destouches was being
carried to an extreme with La Chaussée and his imitators and pro-
voking the wrath of contemporary critics, comedy designed to preserve the traditional comic vein was likewise running the gantlet
of contemporary critics. The majority of critics were of the opinion that the characters capable of portrayal on the stage had been
exhausted and that the depiction of contemporary manners had become so insipid as to be incapable of holding the attention of an
audience without a love complication in the foreground. Harassed
by such distressing circumstances, authors in the last years of the
preceding period and the first years of this period had seen fit to
take refuge, if not in the *larmoyant,* in what critics were pleased

[47] *Journal historique ou Mémoires critiques et littéraires,* 1805, v. 1, année
1750, pp. 234–236, *passim.*
[48] *Ibid.,* p. 238.

to term "faux bel esprit." Neither authors nor critics were long in attacking the weakness of this refuge. Guyot de Merville attributes the success of his *Mascarades amoureuses* (1736) to the fact that

> au milieu du regne de l'affectation et du faux bel-esprit, la simplicité et le vrai avoient encore des Partisans. Des personnages ordinaires, avec la raison et le sentiment, qui sont de tous les tems, de tous les pays et de toutes les conditions, ont plu et touché davantage, que si je leur avois prêté cet esprit *colifichet,* qui, dégradant la raison, semble avoir entrepris de renverser l'ordre de la Nature, et de détruire le génie fondamental du Théâtre. Car, quoiqu'on ne puisse faire d'ouvrage dramatique sans parler, il n'en est pas moins certain, que ce qu'on appelle *la belle conversation* n'est point du ressort de la Comédie, où tout doit être action, de quelque façon qu'elle existe.[49]

Influential critics like Prévost[50] and Desfontaines[51] both approve and reëcho with pleasure this remark of Merville.

It is impossible to ignore in this observation of Merville what seems to be an embarrassing and disconcerting contradiction, one which we have already noted in the thought of De Launay and which we find is generally characteristic of eighteenth century dramatic theory and criticism.[52] In the very same preface that an author expresses his preference for what he usually terms "une intrigue simple et soutenue," he gives vent to the disfavor with which he regards contemporary authors who rely on sparkling conversations rather than on substantial action for the success of their comedies. Critics who in practice invariably condemn contemporary comedy for being "vuide d'action" in theory uphold the "intrigue simple et soutenue" as the ideal of dramatic art. Even the best and most logical of eighteenth century critics, Grimm for example, are not exempt from this contradiction. It seems plausible to attribute this inconsistency to the fact that the question of the importance or unimportance of plot was still in a state of vacillation. Although De Launay and Merville, Prévost and Desfontaines all reflect the tendency toward shifting values, they are still near enough to the seventeenth century to be imbued with the classical

---

[49] Préface, p. 3.   [50] *Le Pour et le contre,* v. 9, 1736, p. 347.
[51] *Observations sur les écrits modernes,* v. 7, 1737, p. 43.
[52] Cf. also, Gaiffe, *op. cit.,* p. 453.

ideal of simplicity and conscious enough of their own relative deficiencies to appreciate the dramatic masterpieces of the preceding
age.[53] They are torn between the inimitable results produced by the
classical ideal and their consciousness of the demands of a new
order. While they seem to believe, as Desfontaines clearly states,
that the simple *comédie de caractère* and *comédie de moeurs* are no
longer tolerable without some action, if it be only an amatory intrigue, nevertheless, theoretically, they are loathe to admit into
comedy anything more than the simplest plot.

The same vacillating state of mind is betrayed by authors who
are waking to the beauties of foreign literatures. We have seen
how Destouches, at the same time that he discredits the irregulari-
ties of English dramatists, looks enviously at the liberties which
they enjoy; in a similar spirit Du Perron de Castera undertakes to
introduce some of the beauties of Spanish comedy to the French
public. He begins by indicating the essential differences between
the dramatic ideals of the two nations and with good orthodox taste
lauds the French public's preference for *comédies de caractère* and
simple subjects devoid of complicated intrigues and innumerable
incidents. Nevertheless he remarks a few pages later that the immense differences between the ideals of the two stages should not
lead his reader to suppose that Spanish plays are without value or
interest for the French author. On the contrary, he will find in
them "beaucoup d'invention, des sentimens nobles et pleins de délicatesse, des caracteres marqués avec force et soutenus avec dignité,
des situations heureuses, des surprises bien ménagées, un grand
fonds de Comique, un feu d'intérêt qui ne laisse point languir le
Spectateur."[54]

A few years later, with less hesitancy, La Place takes up and en-
larges the earlier observation of Prévost and Voltaire that the
English translators and producers of French classical tragedy and
comedy never present them to the English public without having
first increased the plot complications.[55] Concerning the English au-

---

[53] On the classical tendencies and reminiscences of eighteenth century
writers in general cf. P. Moreau, *le Classicisme des romantiques*, 1932, chapter II.
[54] *Théâtre espagnol*, 1738, pp. 8-9.
[55] *Théâtre anglois*, v. 1, 1745, pp. lxviii–lxix.

thor's disregard of the unities La Place concludes, as Lesage had concluded some years earlier concerning Spanish authors,

> si plusieurs actions rassemblées, sans confusion, font plus d'effet qu'une seule; si elles augmentent l'attention et l'intérêt, dûs à la principale, au lieu de les diminuer; si le changement de la Scene, et le transport de l'action, d'un lieu à un autre, présentent de nouveaux Spectacles . . . pourquoi réduire son attention, et ses plaisirs, dans les bornes d'un seul lieu, d'une seule action, et d'une seule journée?[56]

As the *comédie larmoyante* and the comedy which relied on *bel esprit* for its success were criticised for lack of plot, so the psychological studies of Marivaux were frowned on for the same reason. It is not unusual for modern critics to attribute the relative unpopularity of Marivaux's plays to the eighteenth century's inability to comprehend their psychological significance. This is not entirely true for Granet admits that "On sçait assez qu'il n'est point d'Auteur qui possede davantage le métaphysique du coeur, mais les talens déplacés perdent beaucoup de leur mérite. Je souhaiterois qu'il sacrifiât un peu du dialogue à l'action; elle est l'ame du poëme dramatique . . ."[57] This is not an isolated criticism attributable to Granet's individual lack of discrimination but may be considered fairly, although not entirely, representative of contemporary opinion. There appeared the following year in the *Mercure de France* a similar criticism of *les Sincères*. The play was successful at its first appearance and "ne l'auroit pas moins été dans les suivantes, s'il ne falloit que de l'esprit pour faire une bonne Comédie; on a trouvé que l'action n'a pas assés de consistance, et que si l'on retranchoit tout ce qui n'est que conversation, il ne resteroit pas de quoi faire deux ou trois petites Scenes." Although the critic admits that the play had many qualities which deserved applause, he is of the opinion that "rien ne lui a fait plus de tort que le manque d'action" and concludes that "M. de Marivaux sera sûr de réüssir, quand il négligera un peu moins le fond des choses . . ."[58]

[56] For La Place's criticism and interpretation of the English theater in general cf. L. Cobb, *Pierre-Antoine de la Place*, 1928, chapters II, III. According to Miss Cobb, La Place, because of his inability to comprehend fully the psychological import of Shakespeare, "s'attache plus à l'intrigue qu'à autre chose." (P. 39.)

[57] *Réflexions sur les ouvrages de littérature*, 1738, v. 1, p. 181.

[58] Février, 1739, pp. 343–344, 350–351, *passim*.

It is not surprising that the *comédie larmoyante,* the comedy replete with dashes of wit, or the psychological comedies of Marivaux met with opposition; attempts at innovation seldom appear without arousing some adverse criticism. The astonishing thing in this case is that *each of these three distinctly different attempts at innovation met with opposition on the same basis,* namely, lack of sufficient plot. The wave of *sensibilité* which swept over the public of the first half of the century found expression in the *âmes sensibles* of the *comédie larmoyante.* Was the presence of *sensibilité* alone a positive guarantee for the success of this *genre?* The eighteenth century is regarded as the age of sparkling wit and ironic humour. Was the presence of *bel esprit* alone a positive guarantee for the success of a comedy? The more authors lose themselves in filling their comedies with weary narratives necessary to explain too complicated plots, the more they resort to sallies of wit and effervescent conversations, the more do critics clamor for substantial plots and complicated actions.

Even authors like Piron and Gresset whose *Métromanie* and whose *Méchant* according to modern critics[59] possess substantial plot in comparison with the plot of Molière's *comédies de caractère* found little applause on that score when they first appeared. Desfontaines marvels at the genius of an author capable of writing an amusing comedy of five acts "sans intérêt et sans intrigue."[60] And Prévost asserts that many people "surpris de se voir attachés aux représentations, par une intrigue simple et qui n'a point d'apparence sensible d'intérêt, soupçonnoient l'art des Acteurs de leur faire une certaine illusion."[61] An anonymous critic of the *Méchant* finds that

la plûpart des ridicules n'y sont point en action. . . . La Comédie doit peindre les moeurs générales; mais c'est dans des sujets déterminés, dans la conduite et l'action de ses propres personnages . . . et non en maximes, et traits sententieux, en portraits inanimés, en tirades satyriques . . . plus de chaleur dans l'action, et de vraisemblance dans l'intrigue feroient peut-être une Comédie de ce qui ne paroit qu'une espéce de Satyre.[62]

[59] Gaiffe, *op. cit.,* p. 453.
[60] *Observations sur les écrits modernes,* v. 12, 1738, p. 218.
[61] *Le Pour et le contre,* v. 14, 1738, p. 259.
[62] *Lettre sur la comédie du Méchant,* n.d., pp. 3–5, *passim.* Cf. similar criti-

From the point of view of the subsequent evolution in the value assigned to plot and its construction an opinion expressed by Fréron near the end of the period is of the utmost importance. Critics had censured *l'Apparence trompeuse* of Merville because the ending of the play was apparent before the comedy was half finished. Fréron agrees that this is true, but that "selon la judicieuse remarque de M. de Fontenelle, un dénouement prévû par les Spectateur (*sic*) n'est pas défectueux, quand il est imprévu par les Acteurs de la Piéce."[63] Heretofore an unforeseen *dénouement* had been considered the ideal termination for a comedy. Provided there was an element of surprise in the ending of the play, the manner and means of the author for arriving at this *dénouement* seemed to be considered of secondary importance. In this criticism Fréron suggests that a contrary opinion may be admissible and implies that the arrangement of the plot, the incidents leading to its *dénouement,* the bewildering and embarrassing situations in which the characters find themselves, their manner of extricating themselves, with the wires of the whole structure strung together so as to be visible to the audience, but invisible to the characters of the play— in this direction lies a relatively unexplored field. And at this point Fréron almost steps upon the path which leads to Beaumarchais. As we have said, this criticism is merely an implication, a suggestion without development. It is extremely important for us to note this implication, however, so that we shall not be obliged to consider the full expression of it in the succeeding period an isolated, thoughtless opinion, the whim of a moment; we shall be able to state rather that the whole theory was the result of an idea which had been germinating for some time.

Parallel with the increasing value set upon plot we see in the second half of this period the beginning of an active interest in the construction of that plot. On this score Desfontaines sounds the note of warning in his criticism of Boissy's *les Dehors trompeurs*

cism in *Nouvelle lettre écrite de Rome sur la comédie du Méchant,* 1748, and Fréron, *Lettres sur quelques écrits de ce tems,* 1749, v. 1, pp. 13–14.

[63] Desfontaines, *Jugemens sur quelques ouvrages nouveaux,* v. 1, 1744, p. 336. According to Quérard (*la France littéraire,* v. 3, p. 211) Fréron contributed actively to the publication of this periodical. Because of the similarity between this opinion and the one found later in his *Année littéraire,* we have thought it correct to consider him responsible for the opinion expressed here.

when he declares that the spectator is quite indulgent regarding the
verisimilitude of the plays he sees and allows all kinds of supposi-
tions provided they lead to new and amusing situations, but that
"nos Poëtes abusent de cette indulgence."[64] A writer of the *Journal des Savants* is quick to praise Fagan's "art de se renfermer
dans son sujet, de n'emploïer dans le Dialogue de chaque Scéne
que des choses qui ont rapport à l'action."[65] A turbulent *parterre*
which had been criticised for not allowing the actors of the Théâtre
Italien to finish their performance of *le Trésor caché* receives the
support of a critic of the *Mercure* who declares that "il y a des ex-
positions dramatiques si vicieuses qu'on peut décider sans témerité
de l'intrigue et du dénoûment qu'elles dévancent. Il n'est pas nécessaire pour juger de la fabrique d'une étoffe d'en examiner la piéce
entière ; un échantillon suffit aux connoisseurs."[66] Unless an author
gives some attention to the manner in which he puts his plot together, the time is at hand when he need no longer expect the sym-
pathy of the contemporary critic.

As we review the accomplishments of these twenty years of
theory and criticism, two facts stand out above all others. First,
thanks to the efforts of Riccoboni and Destouches to respond in
some positive measure to the displeasure with which contemporary
plays were being regarded, the plot of comedy has been raised to
the same level as that occupied by the characters. The suggestion
of Riccoboni and Destouches appeared rather early in the period
and lest the reader feel skeptical about its influence and doubtful
about its firm acceptance by other writers, we call attention to some
general observations on comedy which appeared at the very end of
the period under consideration. The author of these observations
sums up very nicely the average opinion of his time when he says :

> Les piéces de caracteres sont, avec raison, plus goûtées aujourd'hui
> que les piéces d'intrigue. Celles-ci ne sont que le phantôme de la vérité ;
> celles-là en sont le fidéle tableau. On y voit peints au naturel ceux avec
> qui nous vivons ; au lieu que dans les piéces de pure intrigue, on ne joüit
> que de l'art d'une conduite ingénieuse. Cet art au reste appartient égale-
> ment aux piéces de caracteres ; parce que l'intrigue est la base du genre

[64] *Observations sur les écrits modernes*, v. 21, 1740, p. 134.
[65] 1740, p. 62.   [66] Mars 1745, p. 168.

dramatique. Sans intrigue, point de Comédie. C'est l'intrigue seule qui la distingue du Dialogue. Tous les Drames à la Mosaïque, formés de Scénes rapportées, ne sont donc point des Comédies, mais des Dialogues, souvent insipides, et qui ne peuvent servir qu'à corrompre le goût.[67]

The average eighteenth century critic or author of the end of the period mirrored this change in values even if he were so conservative as to refuse to admit it. For example, a critic of the *Mercure* in connection with *le Faux savant* of Du Vaure wrote: "On s'est plaint de ce que l'intrigue n'étoit pas neuve. Selon quelques Censeurs, les deux derniers Actes sont foibles. . . . Sans doute il y a peu d'invention dans la Fable de la Piéce, mais on n'a pas coûtume d'examiner sévérement sur cet article les Auteurs des Comédies de Caractére."[68] And this bewildered critic apparently fails to realize that by his very response to just such criticism he is admitting its existence.

We have seen, also, how the plot complications and romanesque action admitted to Destouches' scale of values were wrongly and unsuccessfully carried to an extreme in La Chaussée's conception of things and we have intimated what will come out of that failure. As the criticism of Collé proves, a reaction is impending to the mystery enveloping the *intrigue romanesque.* Contemporary writers are beginning to feel that they want not an action which is so complicated that it must be entrusted to long narrations, but rather a plot with threads that will be displayed and woven before their eyes into a well-constructed whole.

The second fact which seems to stand out above all others in this second period of development is that preoccupation with plot has become so great as to threaten the success of any attempt at innovation without it. The dissatisfaction which began in the preceding period of transition has increased during this period to utter contempt for the episodic comedy and to application of severer criticism to the *opéra-comique* and comedies written for the Théâtre Italien. We have seen the sweeping condemnation aroused by writers who sought refuge in *bel esprit;* by dramatists like Marivaux who dared to center their attention on something other than

[67] Fréron, *Lettres sur quelques écrits de ce tems,* 1749, v. 1, p. 5.
[68] Novembre 1749, p. 177.

plot; and by authors like Piron and Gresset who really attempted to respond to the incessant demand. The failure of the continuators of comedy with a frankly gay tone to respond to the increasing demand for plot only aggravated the desire for it and near the end of the period we find a writer like Fréron who is almost willing to attribute the whole value of comedy to an ingenious plot.

In other words, we may safely state that under the accumulating mass of criticism the eighteenth century has ceased to consider the plot of comedy incidental and the construction of that plot is no longer a negligible quality. Although one step has been taken toward the establishment of a new set of values, the ultimate and definitive value which should be assigned to plot is still in the balance. Authors have admitted its importance; they have recognized the potential value in this phase of dramatic art and, for want of something better, they are beginning to appreciate the immediate benefit which its cultivation might bring to contemporary comedy. As yet, however, it has occurred to no one to declare that everything must be subordinated to it.

CHAPTER III

1750–1760

The preface to an anonymous edition of the works of Voisenon; the author's
definition of comedy.—Fréron's indictment of Palissot's *Tuteurs.*—The
theories of Diderot concerning plot and its construction.—The evidence
brought by La Porte.

From the point of view of dramatic production the decade ex-
tending from 1750 to 1760 is relatively devoid of interest. From
the point of view of dramatic theory and criticism this decade offers an especially attractive field for study because it includes at
once an ending and a beginning; an ending in that it marks the
culmination of the efforts of the first half of the century to center
attention on the plot and construction of comedy, a beginning in
that it witnesses the formulation of a criterion which will, to the
practical exclusion of all others, dominate the French stage for the
next fifty-odd years.

When one considers that at this point in the development which
we are tracing criticism is represented by Grimm and Fréron, two
of the eighteenth century's most active and constructive critics, and
by Diderot, the assimilative genius of the century, it is not surprising that theories which we have watched maturing at a cumulative
rate during a half century should come to fruition within the short
space of ten years.

A brief review of the adverse criticism evoked by the comedy of
this decade will show us that the interest in plot which had led in
the preceding years to its elevation in importance to the level of
character-study has not ceased but rather increased in inverse pro-
portion to what was considered lack of action in contemporary
plays. Moreover, a noticeable change is apparent in the tone of
dramatic criticism, that is, the demand for plot is generally accompanied by a more detailed consideration of its technique and construction.

To judge from the negative criticism of the period writers of
comedy either failed to respond in sufficient measure to the previ-

ously expressed demand for plot or they cluttered their plays with too complicated, romanesque actions. Fréron very clearly defines the situation in 1750 when he complains with his contemporaries that comedy is disfigured

> par des intrigues plus romanesques que n'en admet le Théâtre Espagnol, par une tristesse de sujet et de stile, dont les Anglois ont donné quelques modeles, par un jargon plus précieux et plus recherché que celui des Poëtes Italiens, par des caracteres qui n'existent jamais dans la nature, par des dissertations metaphysiques, par des portraits collés les uns aux autres . . .[1]

There appeared three years later in a preface to an anonymous edition of the comedies of Voisenon one of the most scathing criticisms of contemporary comedy and contemporary spectators which we have read. Both Fréron and Grimm laud the author of the invective, the former attributing it to an anonymous author, the latter, to Voisenon himself.[2] From the author's criticism of conditions in general and of the plays in the volume in particular and from his definition of what constitutes dramatic art one can form a distinct idea of the value which the critic of the middle of the eighteenth century was assigning to plot and its construction.

The writer begins by observing that "On reproche aux Auteurs Modernes de sacrifier les fonds aux détails, de donner des scenes vuides d'action, et chargées de portraits, de négliger l'intrigue, et de préferer ce qui est brillant à ce qui est sensé."[3] Who is responsible for this state of affairs?—none other than the spectator who complains of it since a play has no interest for him

> si elle n'est pas un feu d'artifice perpétuel; à peine a-t-on la patience de supporter une exposition; la préparation des évenemens seroit autant de retranché sur les peintures; les situations seroient autant d'obstacles à des conversations. Les Acteurs forcés par les positions des Scenes, à ne dire que ce qu'ils devroient, n'auroient pas le tems de faire assaut d'esprit . . .[4]

---

[1] *Lettres sur quelques écrits de ce tems*, 1750, v. 3, p. 168.
[2] Fréron, *l'Année littéraire*, 1754, v. 4, pp. 217–218. Grimm, *Correspondance littéraire*, v. 2, avril 1754, p. 335.
[3] *Oeuvres de theatre de M.***, 1753, Préface, p. i.
[4] *Ibid.*, pp. i–ii.

Nor has the author of the comedies to which this general preface serves as introduction avoided the errors of his contemporaries for in *les Mariages assorties* the critic sees "un homme qui fait tout ce qu'il peut pour faire des Vers, et qui ne songe gueres à faire des scenes . . . Ses Personnages sont des moralistes froids qui déclament toujours et qui n'agissent presque jamais." On the other hand, *la Coquette fixée* "est écrite plus naturellement; il y a des peintures du monde assez vrayes; on y trouve de temps en temps quelques Scenes théâtrales; le troisième Acte a du mouvement . . ."[5]

What constitutes for our critic the essentials of dramatic art? One should have first of all "un plan bien combiné, qui consiste dans un enchaînement de scenes où l'embarras augmente par degrez jusqu'à ce qu'il se développe aussi naturellement qu'il paroît avoir été amené et se termine par un dénouement qui ne soit ni forcé, ni prévu."[6] To be sure, characters also are an essential part of every good play. Once the characters have been found, however, "il ne s'agit alors que de les mettre en jeu en ménageant des incidens." And his definition of comedy shows to what extent the critic is centering his interest in the incidents of the play rather than in its characters:

> La Comédie n'est autre chose qu'une avanture principale traversée par des évenemens contraires et vraisemblables. C'est la diversité et l'opposition de ces évenemens qui doit servir à faire sortir ces caractéres, et à répandre du plaisant toujours aux dépens des vices et des ridicules . . .[7]

Criticisms such as these directed against the lack of plot in contemporary comedy are legion. We have selected those of Fréron and an anonymous critic as being most completely representative of general opinion and as indicative of the noticeable diminution of interest in character-study, once the most salient aim of comedy, and the substitution instead of the newer interest in plot. When it is a question of classification of *genres,* the average critic does not hesitate to begin his list with the *comédie de caractère.* Fréron, for example, states that "Les Piéces de caractéres doivent sans con-

[5] *Ibid.,* p. vii.   [6] *Ibid.,* p. ii.
[7] *Ibid.,* p. iv.

tredit être mises à la tête. Celles qui consistent dans une intrigue habilement tissue et dénouée obtiennent le second rang . . ."[8] Likewise, Palissot writes in the preface to his *Tuteurs:* "Je sais que les Pièces de caractère telles que le *Tartuffe* et l'*Avare,* sont certainement du genre le plus difficile et le plus parfait. Les Pièces d'intrigue, telles que le *Légataire,* doivent tenir le second rang."[9] Such was the traditional hierarchy from which, theoretically, the eighteenth century critic or author would never consciously deviate when directly presented with the question of the superiority of one *genre* over another. In the middle of the century, after the plot of comedy had come to receive the same attention as character-study, the contemporary critic or author was hampered by the orthodox classification of *genres*. Even at the end of the century, when the *comédie de caractère* had in practice fallen into general desuetude, the superiority of the *comédie de caractère* as a comic *genre* was still maintained. The acceptance of such classification is natural and correct for where is the critic of today who, although he fully appreciates and enjoys the superior technique of the *comédie d'intrigue* perfected by Beaumarchais, will fail to acknowledge the superiority as a *genre* of the *comédie de caractère* perfected by Molière?

The eighteenth century critic's acceptance of the same standard, whenever the occasion presented itself, is perfectly admissible and in no way destroys the thesis which we are attempting to establish. While, theoretically, he still adheres to the superiority of the *comédie de caractère* as a comic *genre,* actually the eighteenth century critic continues to devote less and less attention to the characters of the play he is criticising and more and more attention to the hitherto relatively neglected elements which enter into more perfect dramatic composition. A study of the positive, constructive theory and criticism of this decade should immediately establish the correctness of this assertion and confirm the fact that actually, during the course of this decade, the average writer relegated the interest afforded by the characters of a play to second place and assigned to the plot and its construction supreme importance.

The increasing favor with which the eighteenth century was

[8] *Lettres sur quelques écrits de ce tems,* 1750, v. 3, p. 273.
[9] *Les Tuteurs,* 1755, Préface, p. xix.

continuing to regard the plot of its comedies is well demonstrated
by an anonymous author's response to a suggestion that amatory
plots be omitted from contemporary comedy. Such a procedure
would not only be difficult, he says, but impossible since these
plots

> sont généralement ce qui est trouvé de plus beau, de plus fin dans toutes
> les Pieces de Théatre; chacun en est avide, chacun les suit; tous les
> coeurs sont dans une douce impatience d'en voir le dénouement et la fin.
> Plus ces intrigues sont adroites et impliquées, leur noeud ingénieux;
> plus leur succès est sûr et la séduction certaine.[10]

When this author suggests that a skillful, ingeniously developed
plot is a certain means of attaining success in comedy-writing, he
is not proposing something entirely new for, as we have seen,
Fréron implied in 1744 that an ingenious arrangement of the incidents of a comic plot and the clever presentation of the characters
of a play in bewildering and disconcerting situations offered interesting possibilities to the inventive dramatist. The suggestion dis-
cernible in Fréron's earlier criticism receives full development in
the first half of this decade.

In 1751 Pierre Clément gives a slightly fuller expression to the
opinion implied in Fréron's criticism of 1744 when he says:

> Ce n'est pas toujours sur l'événement d'une Piéce que doit tomber la
> curiosité; dans les sujets historiques, par exemple, on sait à quoi s'en
> tenir; mais c'est le dévelopement qui vous amuse, le jeu des ressorts qui
> aménent cet événement. Dans les sujets feints, . . . vous pourriez avoir
> les deux objets, et par conséquent le double plaisir . . .[11]

It is Fréron himself, however, who gives complete expression
three years later to his earlier point of view when he attempts to
visualize in criticising Palissot's *Tuteurs* the practical application
of the possibilities inherent in the careful construction of an ingenious plot. Fréron's exposition is important not only as a criticism
of Palissot's *Tuteurs* but as a general indictment of the guardian-
ward comedy as practiced during the first half of the eighteenth
century and, indeed, from the time of Molière.

[10] *Essai sur la Comédie moderne*, 1752, pp. 72–73.
[11] *Nouvelles littéraires de la France*, 1751–1753, Lettre IV, 15 mars 1751,
p. 1.

The first act of Palissot's play had been enthusiastically received by the audience; it exposed the character of the three tutors in portraits both "parlans et bien coloriés." In fact, the whole act was "plein d'esprit, de saillies, et sur le ton du vrai comique."[12] The second act, although fired with the same kind of inspiration, was far from attaining the success of the first. Since he can find nothing amiss in the style, Fréron feels obliged to seek elsewhere the cause for the coolness with which the spectators greeted the second act. A comparison of the *Tuteurs* with the English original on which it was modeled leads him to some amazing discoveries.

In the first place, the four tutors of the English play are distinctly different characters; the three tutors of Palissot resemble each other too closely to be interesting; a man who is infatuated with events which happened two thousand years ago is not very different from one who is interested in people who live two thousand leagues away or from one who is avid for news which comes from a similar distance.[13] This, said Fréron, was a serious error on the part of Palissot, but he committed another and graver error which the English author had cleverly avoided. In the latter's play the young hero does not at once attain his end. According to Fréron,

Toutes ses menées, tous ses travestissemens ne réussissent pas au gré de ses desirs. Il est près d'obtenir un des consentemens; il s'en applaudit déja: point du tout; il s'en voit frustré par l'indiscrétion d'un Valet qui vient l'appeller par son vrai nom, tandis qu'il passoit pour un Egyptien . . . Ce Tuteur donnoit tête baissée dans le piège; mais voyant qu'on a voulu le tromper, il n'en est que plus en garde pour l'avenir. L'Amant éprouve ainsi des difficultés de la part des trois autres Gardiens; en sorte qu'il est obligé de changer souvent de batteries: enfin, ce n'est qu'après mille inquiétudes, mille embarras, mille traverses, qu'il vient à bout d'épouser *Mis Delby,* au grand contentement de tous ceux qui ont été témoins des peines qu'il s'est données.[14]

The outcome of the play was, of course, obvious from the beginning; it was certainly within the laws of all probability and all possibility that the hero would outwit the guardians and win their

[12] *L'Année littéraire,* 1754, v. 7, p. 272.
[13] *Ibid.,* pp. 272–273.   [14] *Ibid.,* p. 274.

ward for himself. Did that knowledge lessen interest in the play? Consideration of this question leads Fréron back to his opinion of 1744 to conclude that a tragedy, a comedy,

> n'en est sans doute que meilleure, lorsque le dénoûment n'est pas prévû, et qu'il sort de l'action. Mais ce n'est pas un si grand défaut qu'il soit prévû. *Car ce n'est pas tant le dénoûment qui fait plaisir au Spectateur que les moyens qu'òn employe pour y parvenir. C'est à ces moyens qu'il faut s'attacher; c'est-là l'essentiel et le difficile de l'art dramatique.*[15]

To present his case more forcefully Fréron supposes the concrete example of a young man who, although he is far from having established himself, will, according to dependable predictions, have made his fortune within a period of two years. The success of this young man is consequently foreseen, we are almost certain of it; it is not that which troubles Fréron. He immediately wants to know "comment cet homme fera sa fortune; . . . par quel manège, par quel chemin, par quels degrés il parviendra; quels concurrens il faudra qu'il écarte, quels ressorts il fera jouer, quelles contradictions il aura à essuyer . . ."[16]—that is what arouses one's curiosity in life and at the theater. Fréron wishes dramatists to apply the same criterion to their plays when he tells them that the "dénoûment peut donc être prévû. Mais si vos incidens ne le sont pas, si vous faites naître des obstacles imprévûs à la fois, et naturels, et que votre Héros ou votre Héroïne les surmonte habilement, vous réussirez."[17]

Returning to the particular, Fréron states that to the violation of this principle is due the lack of success of Palissot's *Tuteurs*. Palissot himself has admitted that the *dénouement* can be detected from the first scenes. While Fréron has agreed that that is true, he adds that the critic's chief cause for quarrel with Palissot lies in his having written

> un second Acte sans intrigue, sans noeud quelconque. Son *Damis* forme le projet d'épouser *Julie,* et il l'épouse presque dans la minute; il n'a que la peine de flatter un moment la manie des trois Tuteurs, de se donner tour à tour pour Nouvelliste, pour Antiquaire, pour Voyageur. On le croit sur sa parole; les imbécilles vieillards n'ont aucun doute, aucun

---

[15] *Ibid.,* pp. 274–275. (Italics mine.)
[16] *Ibid.,* p. 275.   [17] *Ibid.,* pp. 275–276.

soupçon; ils sont attrapés l'un après l'autre de la même manière, et li-
vrent leur consentement avec une promptitude et une facilité peu naturelles, et qui, en les supposant telles, ne seroient pas théâtrales.[18]

Thus, with the development which he now gives to a simple suggestion made in 1744, Fréron is the first writer, so far as we have
been able to find, to shift the dominating emphasis of dramatic
theory to the construction of plot and the technical interest afforded by the pure *comédie d'intrigue,* ingeniously composed. His
previous implication becomes here a definite statement. He fore-
sees and points out very clearly to contemporary authors that in the
future the success of a comedy will depend largely upon the arrangement of the plot, the incidents leading to its *dénouement,* the
bewildering and embarrassing situation in which the characters
find themselves, and their manner of extricating themselves. It is
not the ending which gives the spectator greatest pleasure but
rather the devices which the author sets in motion to bring it about;
it is to these contrivances which he should apply all his force; they
constitute the essence and difficulty of dramatic art.

From the point of view of general import it is impossible to overemphasize the significance of Fréron's criticism, especially when
one considers the circumstances by which it was evoked. In the
preface to his *Tuteurs* Palissot states that his play is a modest attempt at a *genre* generally abandoned by contemporary authors;
"une froide Métaphysique entée sur des événemens sans vraisemblance; une morale vuide d'action, avaient pris la place de ce genre
que *Molière* porta parmi nous à son plus haut degré. . . . On en
vint au point de croire hazarder beaucoup en donnant une Comédie
purement comique . . ."[19] Palissot, eager to follow the example
set some years before by Bret in *la Double extravagance,* is inspired to attempt a rehabilitation of the ancient comic *genre* and he
believes that his "tentative a paru donner quelque espérance que le
Public reverrait, avec plaisir un genre que votre bon goût vous a
fait regretter plus d'une fois."[20]

This observation of Palissot is an indication that the popularity
previously enjoyed by the *comédie larmoyante,* the *comédie séri-*

[18] *Ibid.,* p. 276.
[19] *Les Tuteurs,* 1755, Préface, pp. iv–v, *passim.*
[20] *Ibid.,* p. xxv.

euse, is beginning to wane and that a public ever avid for something different will probably welcome a change. Palissot apparently perceived this. Unfortunately, however, he failed to realize that simple reversion to what might have constituted a successful play in 1705 would scarcely satisfy the audience of 1755, although he admits in regard to his own play "qu'il y a loin d'une bonne Comédie à une petite Pièce presque sans noeud et sans intrigue, dont le dénoûment est prévû dès les premières scènes . . ."[21] What he failed to observe, however, Fréron firmly points out in his comparison of the *Tuteurs* with the English original. He expresses displeasure and surprise that Palissot thought it unnecessary to adopt the plot and all the characters of the English original; he believes that of all the young authors who have just entered upon a dramatic career there is no one "qui entende mieux l'art de faire parler ses personnages; il ne lui manque que de sçavoir les faire agir . . ."[22] From the point of view of general importance Fréron's criticism is positive evidence that the rehabilitation of frankly gay comedy, an excellent aim in itself, will henceforth be impossible without a substantial, ingeniously arranged plot as a basis for the play. The characters of a comedy must do something beside talk; they must act.

In addition to its general significance, Fréron's criticism of *les Tuteurs* is of particular importance to anyone interested in the development of the guardian-ward comedy. In the constructive criticism which he offers Fréron points out the flaw in the plot not only of the *Tuteurs* but of every guardian-ward comedy which had graced the French stage from Molière's *l'École des femmes* to the moment with which we are at present concerned. The chief characteristic of the guardian in such comedies is stupidity and unnatural credulity. He falls into the trap set for him by his ward, her lover, or a valet, as the case may be, with what we have seen Fréron term "une promptitude et une facilité peu naturelles, et qui, en les supposant telles, ne seroient pas théâtrales." He points out the superiority in this respect of the English comedy which inspired Palissot; although the tutor here walks blindly into the first trap set for him, he realizes at once that an attempt is being made to deceive him, "il n'en est que plus en garde pour l'avenir," and it

[21] *Ibid.*
[22] Fréron, *op. cit.,* pp. 276–278, *passim.*

is only after "mille inquiétudes, mille embarras, mille traverses" that the hero attains his end.

It hardly seems necessary to point out that, in his criticism of the *Tuteurs,* Fréron anticipates the *Barbier de Séville.* No one can deny that Beaumarchais succeeded perfectly in detecting and correcting the same flaw in the plot of the guardian-ward comedy already indicated by Fréron. It is equally certain that Beaumarchais' detection and rectification of the flaw were not the result of a stroke of unconscious dramatic genius; he was wholly aware of what he was doing. That he acted with definite intention is indicated by his express admission in the *Lettre modérée sur la chute et la critique du Barbier de Séville,* "et de cela seul que le tuteur est un peu moins sot que tous ceux qu'on trompe au théâtre, il a résulté beaucoup de mouvement dans la pièce, et surtout la nécessité d'y donner plus de ressort aux intrigants." Obviously, that is the same remedy which Fréron suggested some twenty years earlier.

Whether Beaumarchais was familiar with the criticism of Fréron is another question. It is impossible to affirm that Beaumarchais read the particular page of the *Année littéraire* on which Fréron expressed his views regarding the *Tuteurs* of Palissot. It is true that from a chronological point of view Beaumarchais is closer to Fréron than to Riccoboni, for example, and the *Année littéraire* until the last years of its existence enjoyed immense popularity and wielded uncontested influence.[23] Likewise, when one considers that in the twenty years intervening between Fréron's criticism and the work of Beaumarchais suggestions of an analogous nature for improving the conventional plot of the guardian-ward comedy were made by writers of no less importance than Grimm, Diderot, and Sedaine, suggestions to which we shall call attention later, one is inclined to believe that Beaumarchais' ingenious plan for vivifying a conventional plot is neither, to use his own words, "l'effet du hasard ni celui d'une boutade heureuse, comme on m'a fait l'honneur de le penser . . ."[24]

One can deduce from this criticism of Fréron, however, a fact

[23] Cf. Cornou, *Elie Fréron,* 1922, also, VanTieghem, P., *l'Année littéraire* (*1754–1790*) *comme intermédiaire en France des littératures étrangères,* 1917, p. 6.
[24] *Essai sur le genre dramatique sérieux,* 1767, p. xxxiii.

of greater importance than the possibility of Beaumarchais' acquaintance with earlier efforts and suggestions for improving the guardian-ward comedy. We have seen how, during the first half of the century, the plot of comedy came to receive the same attention on the part of critics and authors as the characters of a play. With Fréron there is an absolute lack of interest in the characters as such. To be sure, he desires a tutor who will be less credulous, less stupid, not for the sake of verisimilitude or character-study, but rather for the sake of the increased amount of action which will result in the play. He is not interested, as Molière was, in any moral issue which the usual situation of the guardian-ward comedy may present. The tricks which the hero will have to devise, the rival he will have to outwit, the hidden strings he will have to pull, the opposition he will have to overcome—that is what arouses Fréron's interest. And at this point Fréron indicates the reform to be accomplished by Beaumarchais. In other words, Fréron's criticism is evidence that the attitude toward plot and its construction in comedy in general, and in the guardian-ward comedy in particular, has changed; the emphasis has shifted; likewise, an entirely new demand has been made and a new set of values suggested.

Although a new criterion is thus being formed by Fréron, one cannot as yet say that it has been unreservedly established. Grimm's criticism of Palissot's *Tuteurs,* while less interesting than that of Fréron because it is lacking in constructive suggestions, illustrates very clearly that the new set of values has not been definitely accepted. Like Fréron, Grimm bewails the fact that Palissot has shown no talent "pour varier les incidents ou tirer parti de l'intrigue; nul art . . . pour conduire et faire marcher l'action . . ."[25] Unlike Fréron, however, he evidences some interest in the characters of the play and finds "les différents portraits des trois tuteurs trop longs, trop diffus, trop chargés à la vérité, mais cependant (peints) avec un pinceau assez léger et facile . . ."[26] Likewise, he considers the author's method of leaving the description of the principal characters of the play to a *soubrette* an extremely weak device. If Grimm shows some concern for Palissot's lack of plot-technique, he is likewise concerned that he

[25] *Correspondance littéraire,* v. 2, 1754, p. 402.
[26] *Ibid.,* p. 401.

should display "nul art pour faire sortir les nuances d'un caractère . . ."[27]

By 1758 Grimm's point of view has not changed. If he censures
Bret's *le Faux généreux* because "les caractères sont faibles," he
remarks that "le tissu de la pièce l'est aussi." He does not fail to
note "des scènes de remplissage dont tous les actes sont farcis" and
that the play is "remplie de ce qu'on appelle tirades, qu'on applaudit toujours; mais cela ne fait pas marcher l'action."[28] When
criticising *la Coquette corrigée* of La Noue in 1757 Fréron writes
in the same vein which he had used in criticising *les Tuteurs*. It is
inevitable that the aunt will be successful in attaining her end for
the charming qualities possessed by Clitandre will surely touch the
heart of Julie; but, Fréron storms, "La disposition des Actes et
des scènes intermédiaires saute aux yeux; la pièce est sans intrigue,
sans obstacles, sans embarras . . ."[29] He believes that only three
characters are really necessary to the plot; all the others "sont
superflus, et ne tiennent point à la pièce par le plus petit fil; ils n'y
sont que pour le remplissage. Ils viennent et s'en vont sans raisons,
sans motifs, et sur les plus légers prétextes."[30] The following year
he sees in Boissy's *l'Embarras du choix* a "sujet mal choisi et peu
propre à une Comédie, caractères manqués, situations mal amenées
et qui tombent des nues, intrigue extrêmement embrouillée et dénouée par un coup de Théâtre absolument inattendu, scènes mal
coupées, Actes d'une longueur insoutenable . . ."[31]

Such criticisms as these of Fréron and Grimm reflect, to a different degree, an unmistakable shift of emphasis in dramatic
values. In spite of the probable influence exerted by Fréron's original criterion for judging comedy, a criterion which was but the
first adequate expression of a rather common and increasingly evident feeling, one can scarcely consider Fréron the founder of a
new body of dramatic principles. One must be fair and admit that
to whatever excesses Fréron or Grimm might go in acknowledging
on specific occasions the value which should be assigned to plot and
its construction both critics had enough dramatic sense to realize

---

[27] *Ibid.*, p. 402.
[28] *Op. cit.*, v. 3, 1758, pp. 472–473, *passim.*
[29] *L'Année littéraire*, 1757, v. 1, p. 33.
[30] *Ibid.*, p. 34.   [31] *Op. cit.*, 1759, v. 1, p. 19.

that in the highest art everything should not be subordinated to it. To promulgate more widely and to establish more firmly the formula to which Fréron had given expression, to dispel any lingering interest in character-study which a critic like Grimm might arouse (an interest which, of course, both Fréron and Grimm would always theoretically claim), the new principle needed a less cautious, more impulsive, more enthusiastic defender. It found that defender in the author of *le Fils naturel* and *le Père de famille*.

No one becomes more aware of the inconsistencies and contradictions present in Diderot's dramatic theories than the person who attempts to discuss them in a clear, intelligible order. Critics of Diderot generally agree in admitting his predilection for paradoxes and his complete indifference to formulating a body of coherent doctrines. He seems to have had an enormous capacity for assimilation; although his impressionable nature was likely to be influenced by the work of his predecessors, Diderot was at the same time endowed with enough creative genius, enough independence of thought to enable him to give to struggling tendencies a more original, more positive interpretation. It is interesting, if not important or conclusive evidence of his attention to plot, to note that he devotes 50 pages of his *De la Poésie dramatique* to the discussion of dramatic *genres,* 26 to pantomime and costuming, and 102 pages to a detailed study of play-construction.[32] In fact, his dramatic treatises seem definitely to mark the culmination of the efforts of the first half of the century to center attention on plot and its construction. For the first time in the history of French dramatic criticism, everything is subordinated to an intense interest in the construction of a play.

It is not the purpose of this study to present to the reader a complete discussion of the several aspects of Diderot's dramatic theory. Leaving aside his appeal for the acceptance of a new dramatic *genre* and his original ideas for improving its material presentation, his *poétique* will be examined with the hope of explaining some of his hitherto unintelligible statements and of determining his influence upon the subsequent development of dramatic theory.

---

[32] The figures represent round numbers. Diderot rarely confined one page to a single question—extraneous matter invariably entered his discussion.

The majority of Diderot's suggestions concerning dramatic construction seem to have been made with the *drame* in mind. In view, however, of the eighteenth century's growing tendency to destroy the barriers previously existing between dramatic *genres* and to unite openly the comic and the serious, and in view of the fact that Diderot's theories regarding plot and its construction were indifferently applied by subsequent writers to any kind of play, no distinction will be made in the following discussion, unless otherwise stated, between the *genres;* his statements will be considered applicable to drama in general.

Let us examine first of all his attitude toward the relative importance of character and plot. He proclaims of course with the majority of eighteenth century critics, "je fais plus cas d'une passion, d'un caractère qui se développe peu à peu, et qui finit par se montrer dans toute son énergie, que de ces combinaisons d'incidents dont on forme le tissu d'une pièce où les personnages et les spectateurs sont également ballottés."[33]

Think, on the other hand, of his apparently incomprehensible statement, "c'est aux situations à décider des caractères."[34] This statement restricts to an incredible degree the ideal to which he has just subscribed and illustrates the fact that, although at times Diderot may have walked with his head in the clouds, his feet trod none the less upon the common ground of eighteenth century opinion. When Diderot makes this statement, what is he doing if not carrying to its logical conclusion the attitude first assumed by Destouches and adopted later by his successors? He is simply repeating the method of Destouches when he describes thus the current practice in writing *comédie de caractère:* "On cherchait en général les circonstances qui le faisaient sortir, et l'on enchaînait ces circonstances."[35] Once writers had become interested *first* in the plot through which their characters would move and *afterwards* in the characters themselves, it is conceivable that they would mould the characters to fit the plot or, as Diderot says, the situations would determine the characters. Whether or not the eighteenth century was aware of it, this had become the accepted technique for the

---

[33] *De la Poésie dramatique* (1758), p. 316, in *Oeuvres complètes,* ed. by J. Assézat, 1875–1877.
[34] *Ibid.,* p. 347.   [35] *Entretiens,* p. 150. Troisième entretien.

comédie de caractère. Diderot was the first critic to state the case
so baldly. Not only does he admit that in accordance with current
practices of writing comedy the situations *would* determine the
characters, but he goes a step further and proclaims that the situations *should* determine the characters. In this way Diderot completes the work of a half-century.

He only emphasizes his belief in this doctrine by saying: "Le
plan d'un drame peut être fait et bien fait, sans que le poëte sache
rien encore du caractère qu'il attachera à ses personnages."[36] Although we should scarcely go so far as Formentin in justifying
Diderot's statements from an aesthetic point of view,[37] we do not
consider it fair to Diderot to attribute them to utter lack of dramatic sense. It seems preferable to judge them not from an absolute but from a relative point of view, to attribute them to the
forces at work during the first half of the century and to see in
them the deplorable, yet absolutely true expression, not only of the
tendencies of contemporary theory, but of contemporary practice.
The secondary dramatists of the period were neither capable nor
desirous of creating characters of sufficient force to determine the
action of a play. Could not Beaumarchais himself have formed the
plan for his *Barbier de Séville* before he had definitely decided
about the character of his players? One needs only to witness the
presentation of this comedy by different groups of actors to appreciate what little variation is to be found in all the characters, Figaro excepted, and what little chance for characterization seems to
be offered to the actor. Figaro appears to be the only rôle which
lends itself to different interpretations. And does Figaro himself
attain that quality of universality which we usually attribute to a
dramatic character, to Harpagon, for example? Is he not rather the
pure incarnation of his author's *esprit?* With an egoism which approaches that of the Romantic writers Beaumarchais delights in
projecting his own personality on the stage. That his own distinguishing characteristic should assume living form is of more inter-

[36] *De la Poésie dramatique*, p. 347. While Diderot, at the beginning of his
own work, refers with great respect to Aristotle, it is difficult to determine
the extent to which he was aware of the meaning of Aristotle's ideas on the
supremacy of plot. (*De Poetica*, ch. 6, *passim*.) It is possible that he uninten-
tionally misinterpreted these views or found it useful to revamp them.
[37] *Essai sur les origines du drame moderne en France*, 1879, pp. 83–84.

est to him than the psychological study of a given character's reactions to a given situation. The possible identity of Molière with Alceste does not lessen the fact that Alceste is *the* misanthropist *par excellence*. Figaro is Beaumarchais and Beaumarchais alone.

Nevertheless one must acknowledge that Diderot's complete subordination of character to plot was not entirely without qualification; one cannot ignore in this connection his famous theory of substituting the study of conditions for that of character.[38] His interest in "conditions," however, is far from destroying his interest in the plot surrounding the person who represents the "condition." Suppose that someone proposes to portray on the stage the "condition" of judge. After having stated the proposition, the first thing which comes to Diderot's mind in regard to what the poet must do is "qu'il intrigue son sujet d'une manière aussi intéressante qu'il le comporte et que je le conçois . . ."[39] What is the most valid objection which he can imagine to his suggestion for making "conditions" the subject of a play? None other than can one

renfermer, dans les bornes étroites d'un drame, tout ce qui appartient à la condition d'un homme? Où est l'intrigue qui puisse embrasser cet objet? On fera, dans ce genre, de ces pièces que nous appelons à tiroir; des scènes épisodiques succéderont à des scènes épisodiques et décousues, ou tout au plus liées par une petite intrigue qui serpentera entre elles: mais plus d'unité, peu d'action, point d'intérêt.[40]

We have watched Diderot subordinate his interest in characters to his interest in the external circumstances of a play; we have noted that his main concern for the *drame* is that it must not, in presenting "conditions," become an episodic play without plot, without unity of action, without interest. This same concern for plot is further manifested by a very definite restriction of the moral aim which Diderot held should be latent in every *drame*. He believes that one can discuss "au théâtre les points de morale les plus importants, et cela sans nuire à la marche violente et rapide de l'action dramatique."[41] How will the dramatist accomplish this? He will have only to "disposer le poëme de manière que les choses y fussent amenées," for "Si une telle scène est nécessaire, si elle

[38] Troisième entretien, p. 150.
[40] *Ibid.*, p. 309.
[39] *De la Poésie dramatique*, p. 311.
[41] *Ibid.*, p. 313.

tient au fonds, si elle est annoncée et que le spectateur la désire, il
y donnera toute son attention, et il en sera bien autrement affecté
que de ces petites sentences alambiquées, dont nos ouvrages modernes sont cousus."[42] Again he is subordinating to an artistic construction the social and moral utility which may be derived from a
play when he says,

> Qu'un auteur intelligent fasse entrer dans son ouvrage des traits que le
> spectateur s'applique, j'y consens; qu'il y rappelle des ridicules en
> vogue, des vices dominants, des événements publics; qu'il instruise et
> qu'il plaise, mais que ce soit sans y penser. Si l'on remarque son but, il
> le manque; il cesse de dialoguer, il prêche.[43]

While there seems to be little doubt that Diderot did not wish
the plot of a play to be subordinated to its moral aim, his attitude
toward the question of simplicity versus complexity of plot is less
clearly defined. He affirms, of course, that he prefers the ancients'
conception of a "conduite simple, une action prise le plus près de
sa fin, pour que tout fût dans l'extrême; une catastrophe sans cesse
imminente et toujours éloignée par une circonstance simple et
vraie . . ."[44] He likewise exclaims: "O mon ami, que la simplicité
est belle! Que nous avons mal fait de nous en éloigner!"[45] In such
sentences as these, Diderot is subscribing with the usual banality
to the regretted ideal of a former age. In spite of the fact that he
believes he prefers a simple plot to one overburdened with incidents, he admits elsewhere that he looks more closely "à leur liaison qu'à leur multiplicité." He is less disposed to believe "deux
événements que le hasard a rendus successifs ou simultanés, qu'un
grand nombre qui, rapprochés de l'expérience journalière, la règle
invariable des vraisemblances dramatiques, me paraîtraient s'attirer
les uns les autres par des liaisons nécessaires."[46] The growing interest which we have noted throughout the first half of the century
in perfecting the construction of plot reaches its climax with the
stand taken by Diderot. The question of simplicity versus complexity of plot has virtually ceased to be a question for Diderot; he
adopts the broader point of view by assigning supreme value not to

[42] *Ibid.*, p. 314.
[44] *Ibid.*, p. 316.
[46] Premier entretien, p. 88.

[43] *Ibid.*, pp. 345–346.
[45] *Ibid.*, p. 339.

the simplicity or complexity of a given plot but to the perfection of its mechanical construction.

Whether the poet write in verse or in prose, the very first thing which he should do, according to Diderot, is to make a plan for his play.[47] He exclaims enthusiastically: "Quel ouvrage, qu'un plan contre lequel on n'aurait point d'objection !"[48] It is the dramatist's arrangement of the subject-matter rather than the choice of the subject itself which should elicit admiration for "Le sujet appartient à tous; mais le poëte disposera du reste à sa fantaisie; et celui qui aura rempli sa tâche de la manière la plus simple et la plus nécessaire, aura le mieux réussi."[49] Diderot recognizes, however, that not everyone has the talent necessary for devising ingenious plot constructions. A dramatist who knows and has observed men may still find difficulty in constructing the plan for his play. Another dramatist, who has an imaginative mind, who has devoted much time to the study of poetics, who is thoroughly familiar with the theater, and to whom experience and a certain innate sense have suggested dramatic situations and the clever combination of incidents, will easily construct the plan for his play; its dialogue will probably be his chief stumbling block. Diderot is the first[50] French critic, so far as we have been able to discover, to distinguish clearly between these two types of dramatic genius and, what is really astonishing, he does not value one type of dramatist more highly than the other; he states simply, "l'un et l'autre sont l'ouvrage du génie; mais le génie n'est pas le même." He concludes, however, and the conclusion was valid at the time it was written, that, in general, "il y a plus de pièces bien dialoguées que de pièces bien conduites. Le génie qui dispose les incidents, paraît plus rare que celui qui trouve les vrais discours. Combien de belles scènes dans Molière! On compte ses dénoûments heureux."[51]

It was Diderot's implicit faith in the power of good play-construction which enabled him to state that the poet might have the plan for his play well in mind before he had at all determined the

[47] *De la Poésie dramatique*, p. 322.
[48] *Ibid.*, p. 327.   [49] *Ibid.*, p. 323.
[50] In a discussion on tragedy published in the same year as *De la Poésie dramatique* Piron evidences an analogous point of view, but does not develop it as fully. (Cf. Introduction, pp. 3-4.)
[51] *De la Poésie dramatique*, pp. 319–320.

characters. He even goes so far as to say that the dramatist should not indulge any native talent which he may have for portraying characters. If dramatists think of their characters before they think of the construction of their plot, what happens?

> Ils écrivent, ils écrivent; ils rencontrent des idées fines, délicates, fortes même; ils ont des morceaux charmants et tout prêts: mais lorsqu'ils ont beaucoup travaillé, et qu'ils en viennent au plan, car c'est toujours là qu'il en faut venir, ils cherchent à placer ce morceau charmant; ils ne se résoudront jamais à perdre cette idée délicate ou forte; ils feront le contraire de ce qu'il fallait, le plan pour les scènes qu'il fallait faire pour le plan.[52]

It is on similar grounds that Diderot objects to his contemporaries' predilection for contrasting characters, a method of procedure prevalent in comedy of the first half of the century, and one which, as we have seen, met with the approval of Destouches. Diderot admits that dramatists had resorted to contrasting characters in order to emphasize their qualities or their faults. Obviously, this effect will be obtained in the measure in which these characters appear on the stage together. But Diderot objects,

> quelle monotonie pour le dialogue! quelle gêne pour la conduite! Comment réussirai-je à enchaîner naturellement les événements et à établir entre les scènes la succession convenable, si je suis occupé de la nécessité de rapprocher tel personnage de tel autre? Combien de fois n'arrivera-t-il pas que le contraste demande une scène, et que la vérité de la fable en demande une autre?[53]

Moreover, in the name of decent play-construction Diderot protests against the practice of adjusting a rôle to suit an actor; in his opinion, "C'est à l'acteur à convenir au rôle, et non pas au rôle à convenir à l'acteur. Qu'on ne dise jamais de vous, qu'au lieu de chercher vos caractères dans les situations, vous avez ajusté vos situations au caractère et au talent du comédien."[54]

Finally, Diderot subordinates to a rigorous technique the poet's spontaneity and rush of inspiration. He recognizes the fact that the gift of imagination distinguishes the man of genius from his fellows; nevertheless, "le poëte ne peut s'abandonner à toute la fou-

---

[52] *Ibid.,* pp. 321–322.   [53] *Ibid.,* p. 349.   [54] *Ibid.,* p. 361.

gue de son imagination; il est des bornes qui lui sont prescrites."
Let the poet give free rein to his imagination and pile up "circonstances bizarres sur circonstances bizarres; j'y consens." He must
not forget, however, that he will have to "racheter tout ce merveilleux par une multitude d'incidents communs qui le sauvent et qui
m'en imposent."[55] Once the poet has formed the outline for his
play,

> qu'il travaille; qu'il commence par la première scène, et qu'il finisse par
> la dernière. Il se trompe, s'il croit pouvoir impunément s'abandonner à
> son caprice, sauter d'un endroit à un autre, et se porter partout où son
> génie l'appellera. Il ne sait pas la peine qu'il se prépare, s'il veut que son
> ouvrage soit un. . . . Les scènes ont une influence les unes sur les autres,
> qu'il ne sentira pas. . . . Le désordre de sa manière de faire se répandra
> sur toute sa composition; et, quelque soin qu'il se donne, il en restera
> toujours des traces.[56]

Diderot does not limit his interest in plot-construction to extravagant praise of its value. With a practical end in view, he describes the special skill which dramatists should cultivate to ensure
a well-constructed plot and he completes his exposition by several
detailed, original suggestions for improving the methods of plot-
technique current in his time.

In order to attain the skill necessary for good plot-construction,
the author has only to "consulter l'ordre et l'enchaînement des
choses; ne pas redouter les scènes difficiles, ni le long travail; entrer par le centre de son sujet; bien discerner le moment où l'action
doit commencer; savoir ce qu'il est à propos de laisser en arrière;
connaître les situations qui affectent . . ."[57]

Perhaps Diderot's greatest contribution to plot-technique was
his insistence that the poet make adequate preparation for the incidents of his play. This idea in itself was by no means new. Saint-
Foix, in the prologue to his *Deucalion et Pirrha,* given for the first
time in 1741, states: "il faut préparer, établir son sujet, filer des
Scènes, des incidens; tenir toujours l'esprit du Spectateur en sus-
pens . . ." In a treatise on the theater translated from the English
in 1750, a critic finds that the most common defects in comedy as
it was then practiced are due to the fact that "les bienséances n'y

---

[55] *Ibid.,* pp. 334–335.   [56] *Ibid.,* pp. 335–336.   [57] *Ibid.,* p. 321.

sont pas gardées, ni les incidens assez préparés."[58] With no other author, however, does the idea occur and reoccur with the same frequency as with Diderot. He gives to the idea the expansion necessary to impose it upon contemporary authors.

The prime requisite in preparing one's incidents is that they be linked one to the other. To use Diderot's own words: "L'art dramatique ne prépare les événements que pour les enchaîner; et il ne les enchaîne dans ses productions, que parce qu'ils le sont dans la nature."[59] And again, in the *De la Poésie dramatique,*—"que des fils imperceptibles lient tous vos incidents."[60] Indeed, for Diderot, the art of constructing a plot "consiste à lier les événements, de manière que le spectateur sensé y aperçoive toujours une raison qui le satisfasse."[61] On the other hand, the dramatist should not overdo his preparation for subsequent events. Diderot warns him that he must not give any false leads; they are likely to interest the spectator in a difficult situation which never arises and thus distract his attention from the point at issue. This careful preparation for subsequent events should begin with the first act; it is necessary that this act "entame, qu'il marche, quelquefois qu'il expose, et toujours qu'il lie."[62]

Diderot's belief in the beneficent results to be obtained by careful preparation of the events of a play is much akin to the formula which, according to M. DesGranges, animated the work of Scribe and his successors: "J'ai l'intime conviction qu'avec l'art des préparations on peut tout mettre au théâtre."[63] M. DesGranges attributes the first expression of this formula to Alexandre Duval, but when Duval says, "il ne faut pas s'effrayer des difficultés que peut offrir un sujet; qu'avec des précautions, on peut tout dire et qu'à la scène comme dans le monde, l'adresse est un moyen de réussir,"[64] or, when he says, *"Les trois quarts des scènes à effet qui sont repoussées par le public, n'ont souvent manqué que de préparation. On ne conçoit pas combien ces préparations sont nécessaires*

---

[58] *Le Theatre ouvert au public ou Traité de la tragédie et de la comédie.* Paris, 1750, p. 169.

[59] Second entretien, p. 130.   [60] P. 327.

[61] Premier entretien, p. 88.   [62] *De la Poésie dramatique,* p. 355.

[63] *Geoffroy et la critique dramatique sous le Consulat et l'Empire,* 1897, p. 441.

[64] Cited by DesGranges, *op. cit.,* p. 442.

. . .,"[65] he is striking a note which was certainly not unknown to Diderot. In fact, Diderot was so convinced of the truth of this idea that he flattered himself into believing he had actually succeeded in putting it into practice. Bret had suggested in a letter to Diderot that he change the plan of his play, presumably *le Père de famille;* so carefully, however, had Diderot prepared for everything in the play, that such a change was unthinkable; the play "est cousu de manière, cette charpente assemblée de façon, que je n'en peux pas arracher un point, déplacer une cheville, que tout ne se renverse."[66]

Diderot's second suggestion for the improvement of plot-technique arises out of the distinction which he makes between the historian and the dramatist. While the former limits himself to a simple presentation of facts, the latter imagines events with which to embellish the facts. The embellishment of historical facts with imaginative events is quite permissible, for, if "le poëme est bien fait, il intéresse tout le monde . . ." Provided the episodes are logically introduced and developed the spectator will enjoy them since they thus become "des mensonges mêlés à des vérités avec tant d'art, qu'il n'éprouve aucune répugnance à les recevoir."[67] In other words, the dramatist must remember one very important thing, namely, that his work may be "merveilleux, sans cesser d'être vraisemblable." In order to produce such a work he has only to conform to the order of nature "lorsqu'elle se plaît à combiner des incidents extraordinaires, et à sauver les incidents extraordinaires par des circonstances communes."[68] Again, a few pages later, Diderot reverts to the same idea of mingling extraordinary events with ordinary details of every day occurrence. The dramatist may unbridle his imagination and transport himself to the realm of extraordinary happenings but the more "ces cas seront rares et singuliers, plus il lui faudra d'art, de temps, d'espace et de circonstances communes pour en compenser le merveilleux et fonder l'illusion."[69] The judgment of the discerning critic will convince the dramatist that "l'oubli le plus léger suffit pour détruire

---

[65] *Ibid.*
[66] Busnelli, *Diderot et l'Italie,* 1925, p. 92, note 1. This unpublished letter of Diderot was first called to the attention of the public by M. R. Cru in *Diderot as a Disciple of English Thought,* 1913, Appendix I, p. 472 f.
[67] *De la Poésie dramatique,* pp. 331–332.
[68] *De la Poésie dramatique,* p. 332.   [69] *Ibid.,* p. 335.

toute illusion; qu'une petite circonstance omise ou mal présentée décèle le mensonge . . ."[70] This suggestion of Diderot proved to be unusually profitable. The success of Sedaine, the success of Beaumarchais, the successes of Scribe and his school were due in large measure to their authors' extreme attention to small details of plot-construction.

Diderot's third suggestion for the improvement of plot-technique is addressed especially to writers of comedy. Not only must the dramatist give careful attention to preparing for the events of his play, not only must he feel free to balance extraordinary events by less important ones, but he should strive for some ingenuity in the devices which he uses in developing his plot. "La tragédie," says Diderot, "demande de l'importance dans les moyens; la comédie de la finesse." Suppose that a jealous lover is uncertain of his lady's feelings. It was all right for Terence to leave on the stage "un Dave qui écoutera les discours de celui-ci (le rival), et qui en fera le récit à son maître." The French spectators of today, however, "voudront que leur poëte en sache davantage."[71] Or, suppose that a vain, stupid, old guardian changes his bourgeois name of Arnolphe to something like Monsieur de la Souche, and suppose that this ingenious expedient forms the basis of a plot and leads to a natural, unexpected *dénouement*. The spectators may cry, "Bravo!" and rightly.

> Mais si, sans aucune vraisemblance, et cinq ou six fois de suite, on leur montre cet Arnolphe devenu le confident de son rival et la dupe de sa pupille; allant d'Horace à Agnès, et retournant d'Agnès à Horace, ils diront: Ce n'est pas un drame, que cela; c'est un conte: et si vous n'avez pas tout l'esprit, toute la gaieté, tout le génie de Molière, ils vous accuseront d'avoir manqué d'invention . . .[72]

Is it likely that Beaumarchais, one of Diderot's ardent supporters, overlooked this suggestion?

Diderot's next hint to the dramatist for improving the plot of his play, a hint reminiscent of Fréron's criticism in connection with *les Tuteurs*, is to remember that the twenty-four hours through which his characters are about to live are the most agitated, the most cruel of their lives. "Tenez-les donc dans la plus grande gêne

[70] *Ibid.*, p. 347.   [71] *Ibid.*, pp. 326–327.   [72] *Ibid.*, p. 327.

possible. Que vos situations soient fortes; opposez-les aux caractères; opposez encore les intérêts aux intérêts. Que l'un ne puisse tendre à son but sans croiser les desseins d'un autre; et que tous occupés d'un même événement, chacun le veuille à sa manière."[73] This demand for play and interplay of action was relatively new; it is a nice example, too, of how completely Diderot's interest has shifted from the psychological study of one or more characters to the external events through which they will move, and how surely his interest in plot must be considered coexistent with any of his other avowed interests in the theater.

We come now to the most original, perhaps, of Diderot's suggestions for changing accepted methods of plot structure. It is all very well to tell an author to keep his characters in an eternal state of vigilance, to confront them with perplexing problems and embarrassing situations. To what extent should he conceal from the spectator, to what extent should he reveal to the spectator the disconcerting situations into which his characters will be led by their own actions or the actions of another? Diderot's solution to the problem of the relative value of surprise and suspense, new for the time, shows at once the originality of his mind and the extremes to which his original ideas were likely to lead him.

He begins conservatively by saying: "si le poëte nous cache assez de ses ressorts pour nous piquer, il nous en laisse toujours apercevoir assez pour nous satisfaire."[74] It is not long, however, before we hear him proclaim pompously: ". . . je ne croirais pas me proposer une tâche fort au-dessus de mes forces, si j'entreprenais un drame où le dénoûment serait annoncé dès la première scène, et où je ferais sortir l'intérêt le plus violent de cette circonstance même."[75]

This exaggeration of an idea in itself commendable seems more comprehensible when one considers its probable source. We remember Collé's indictment of the shroud of mystery in which the characters of the *comédie larmoyante* moved and lived and we found that his condemnation was but one manifestation of a general feeling of resentment prevalent at the end of the first half of the century. M. Lanson, also, objects in criticising *Mélanide* to La Chaussée's exaggerated "surprise" technique when he says, ". . .

---

[73] *Ibid.,* pp. 347–348.   [74] *Ibid.,* p. 328.   [75] *Ibid.,* p. 341.

au théâtre, ce que le bâtard ignore, je dois le savoir, moi, spectateur; et si Mélanide a droit comme Clara Vignot de ne rien dire à son fils, La Chaussée a le devoir de tout découvrir au public comme M. Dumas fils."[76] It is to Diderot's credit that he saw the error in La Chaussée's method of procedure as clearly as Dumas *fils*. His suggestion for changing it is an implicit criticism of the prevailing mode. One cannot believe otherwise when he says: "Tout doit être clair pour le spectateur. Confident de chaque personnage, instruit de ce qui s'est passé et de ce qui se passe, il y a cent moments où l'on n'a rien de mieux à faire que de lui déclarer nettement ce qui se passera."[77] Until the very end, nothing in the typical *comédie larmoyante* was clear to the spectator; he was left in ignorance of the real relationship of one character to another, of what had happened before the opening of the play and what would happen before it ended. Diderot's evident desire to establish a very different kind of plot-technique undoubtedly led him to the confident assertion that an interesting play could be written in which every single event, *dénouement* included, would be announced in the first scene. Given the desire already manifested by the eighteenth century for something different, given Diderot's natural tendency toward the extreme solution to any problem, his answer to the question of surprise versus suspense is exactly what one would expect: in fact, one might almost say that it is logical.

Diderot's demand for suspense rather than surprise as the more perfect means for developing a plot was fortified by sane reasoning. If the mutual relationships and situations of the several characters of a play are unknown to the spectator, he cannot take any more interest in the action than the characters themselves. If, however, he is well aware of what is imminent, his interest will be doubly increased. Since he will realize that the actions and words of the characters would be quite different if they knew as much about each other as he knows about them, he will be consumed with a desire to learn what will happen to the characters when they compare what they are doing with what they did or intended to do.[78] And so Diderot concludes:

Que le spectateur soit instruit de tout, et que les personnages s'igno-

---

[76] *Op. cit.*, p. 183.   [77] *Ibid.*, p. 341.   [78] *Ibid.*, p. 343.

rent s'il se peut; que satisfait de ce qui est présent, je souhaite vivement
ce qui va suivre; qu'un personnage m'en fasse désirer un autre; qu'un
incident me hâte vers l'incident qui lui est lié; que les scènes soient
rapides; qu'elles ne contiennent que des choses essentielles à l'action, et
je serai intéressé.[79]

Finally, the last part of this sentence contains the germ of Diderot's sixth suggestion for the improvement of plot-construction,
namely, the need for accelerated, concentrated action. Not only
should the action of a play be clear, but it should increase in
rapidity as it approaches its end.[80] Stated more concretely, Diderot
sees the action as "une masse qui se détache du sommet d'un
rocher: sa vitesse s'accroît à mesure qu'elle descend, et elle bondit
d'espace en espace, par les obstacles qu'elle rencontre."[81] In order
to obtain this effect, the dramatist must not dream of interrupting
the natural course of the main action with episodic intrigues concerning *valets* and *soubrettes*.

Everyone is aware of Diderot's desire to rid the French stage of
episodic scenes devoted to the intrigues of servants; opposition to
such scenes becomes a matter of course after the publication of his
dramatic treatises. To be sure, the idea is not original with Diderot. In 1737, for example, when criticising *l'Enfant prodigue*, Contant d'Orville remarks that Madame Croupignac is announced by a
valet "(qui) coupe l'intérêt, et fait languir la Scène . . ." and
from whom "on ne peut tirer aucun éclaircissement de ce qu'il doit
dire: écart," adds d'Orville, "qui n'est pas certainement pardonnable, malgré la risée que l'Auteur espéroit tirer ce cette prétendue
situation."[82] In 1741 Saint-Foix had the ingenious idea of composing a play in which there were but two characters and reducing
the usual action to the hero and heroine. Although he admits that
his project was rather difficult to accomplish, he is convinced that
"cet intérêt, ce noeu, ce dénouement qui se trouvent précisément et
uniquement réduits et renfermés entre Pirrha et Deucalion . . .
paroissent heureusement imaginés . . ."[83] The *frères* Parfaict in
1748 add their bit to the idea of eliminating from comedy unneces-

---

[79] *Ibid.*   [80] *Ibid.*, p. 346.   [81] *Ibid.*, p. 319.
[82] *Lettre critique sur la Comédie intitulée l'Enfant Prodigue ou l'Ecole de la Jeunesse*, 1737, p. 23.
[83] *Oeuvres de théâtre*, 1748, *Deucalion et Pirrha*, 1741, Prologue.

sary detail. It is their belief that the remarks "que le critique fait
sur les Valets de cette Comédie (*le Jaloux désabusé*), tendent à
prouver qu'ils sont presque inutiles, et qu'ils servent peu à l'intrigue."[84] These examples will suffice to indicate that here and there
before the *Entretiens* the eighteenth century was beginning to feel
the need for concentrated action and was interested enough to advance concrete suggestions for the elimination of extraneous matter introduced by the typical *valet* or *soubrette*. The expansion of
this same idea in a treatise devoted to dramatic art was all that
was necessary to impose it upon a sympathetic public.

Such, then, is the interest manifested by Diderot in the plot and
construction of a play. We have seen (1) how he subordinates his
interest in the characters of a play to his interest in its construction,
(2) how he restricts the moral aim of the theater by aesthetic considerations, (3) how he gives equal measure of praise to the
dramatist capable of producing a perfectly constructed plot, (4)
how his interest in play-construction leads him to disapprove of the
current practice of contrasting characters, (5) how he protests
against the writer who will disfigure the construction of a plot to
please a popular actor, and (6) how he is inclined to control and
check the spontaneity of the gifted dramatist for the sake of
studied play technique. We have seen, too, how his interest in plot
and its construction leads him to formulate methods for its improvement by contemporary authors. His suggestions that the
dramatist devote a large part of his time (1) to preparing for the
events of his play, (2) to balancing extraordinary events by apparently insignificant details, (3) to striving for some ingenuity
in the arrangement of successive incidents, (4) to keeping his characters in a constant state of turmoil by the play and interplay of
action, (5) to replacing the surprise technique by one of suspense,
and (6) to accelerating and concentrating the action of his play by
the elimination of extraneous material, are practical and valid
enough, as we shall see later, to have been adopted almost *in toto*
by Beaumarchais.

Diderot's originality is thus shown in his insistence on those
phases of dramatic art which, in spite of the very real advances
made before his time, had received only secondary and sporadic

[84] *Histoire générale du théâtre français,* 1748, v. 15, p. 40.

attention; he forces the thought of the century into a new channel by shifting the emphasis of dramatic theory from the portrayal of character to the situations in which the characters find themselves. In other words, *forme* replaces *fond* as the dominant interest of dramatic art. As we have seen, however, this shift in emphasis must not be wholly attributed to Diderot; he was simply carrying to its logical conclusion an hypothesis already more than partially demonstrated by his predecessors.

On the other hand, although it is my belief that, in general, Diderot's theories regarding plot and its construction present a body of doctrine, the intrinsic value of which is equal to that of any of his other theories, these theories may not necessarily have been for him the most important part of his *poétique*. Diderot may not have deliberately planned, nor even wholly foreseen, the ultimate effect which his *credo* might have upon subsequent dramatic theory. That admission, however, does not lessen the importance of the point of view which he consciously or unconsciously adopted. And we have based our conclusions, not upon three or four or five pages of Diderot, but upon a disquieting array of statements which present a fairly consistent whole, a whole to which Diderot adhered as consistently, perhaps more consistently than to any one of his other dramatic opinions.

Whatever the intrinsic value of Diderot's theories may be, they are important for our purposes here only in so far as they influenced the thought of his contemporaries. While it is possible that Diderot's ideas concerning the subject-matter of the new *genre*[85] and the material presentation of a play[86] may have been definitely lost to the early nineteenth century theater or temporarily submerged because of unsettled political conditions at the end of the century, the ideas which we discussed above seem to have had an enduring and quite perceptible influence upon his contemporaries

[85] The opinion of modern critics varies all the way from that of Ducros for whom the theories of Diderot had little or no influence (Ducros, *Diderot, l'homme et l'écrivain*, 1894, p. 271) to that of Reinach who sees in Diderot's theories the origin of early nineteenth century drama. (Reinach, Joseph, *Diderot*, 1894, p. 145.)

[86] Although Miss Melcher admits that in Diderot's theories can be found nearly all of the early nineteenth century's reforms in scenic development, she believes his actual influence in this respect was negligible until a much later time. (Melcher, Edith, *Stage Realism in France between Diderot and Antoine*, 1928, pp. 19–29.)

and his successors. It is in virtue of this fact that they take their place among the most important of his theories.

From 1759 until the beginning of the nineteenth century Diderot's suggestions regarding the importance of plot-construction were approved in general, disapproved occasionally, cited, plagiarized and taken as a standard by which to judge contemporary comedy. One could probably show, too, that a conscious, although not always successful, attempt to put them into practice was made by contemporary dramatists and their successors. The following examples, chosen over a fairly extended period of time, will illustrate the influence exerted by Diderot.

A contemporary critic of the *Mercure* approves of Diderot's advice to the author to form a plan for his play although he does not think this should necessarily precede his conception of the characters, he agrees that the suggestion for balancing extraordinary events by ordinary incidents is an ingenious idea and acknowledges that the contrasting of characters has been exaggerated but should not therefore be excluded.[87]

While Fréron's criticism of *De la Poésie dramatique* as a whole is not very favorable, he emphasizes Diderot's objection to contrasting characters and his call for play and interplay of action: "M. *Diderot* veut que les caractères contrastent avec les situations; que l'on oppose les intérêts aux intérêts; que l'un ne puisse tendre à son but sans traverser les desseins d'un autre, et que tous occupés d'un même événement, chacun le veuille à sa manière. Cette règle me paroît juste et bien présentée."[88]

In 1763 a critic of the *Mercure* lauds a play of Goldoni as producing that endless pleasure and surprise "que donne cette fécondité du plus rare génie, qui dispose des incidens si nécessaires, si propres d'ailleurs à intriguer, qu'il est impossible que les Personnages ne se trouvent pas dans les situations comiques, souvent intéressantes, et toujours vives, où l'Auteur les présente."[89]

The *Encyclopédie* in 1765[90] notes that most critics "exigent que le poëte comique fasse contraster les caracteres pour donner plus de

---

[87] *Mercure de France,* février 1759, pp. 86–94, *passim.*
[88] *L'Année littéraire,* 1761, v. 5, pp. 21–22.
[89] *Mercure de France,* décembre 1763, p. 181.
[90] Date assigned to vol. 8 by Rocafort, *les Doctrines littéraires de l'Encyclopédie,* 1890, p. 14.

saillie au caractere qu'il veut peindre. Mais (M. Diderot) . . . remarque, avec beaucoup de sagacité, que le contraste doit être, non dans les différens caracteres, mais dans les situations."[91] Nougaret[92] and Mercier, too,[93] both sanction a similar principle, the latter, however, applying it exclusively to the *drame*. Nougaret reflects upon the possibility of developing a plot by means of suspense rather than surprise and decides that the former, although not impossible, would be the more difficult technique.[94]

In the *Mercure* for 1768 the *Fausses infidélités* of Barthe is looked upon with favor because the action "n'est jamais retardée par des accessoires étrangers; point de scène épisodique, point d'ornemens superflus: . . . Ce qui caractérise encore cet ouvrage, c'est l'absence des valets et des soubrettes . . ."[95]

In his *De l'Art de la Comédie* Cailhava approves and quotes at length Diderot's opinion regarding the contrasting of characters.[96] Cailhava sounds, too, as if he were reiterating Diderot's opinion concerning the play and interplay of action when he hints that the incidents of a comedy

> ont beau naître d'un sujet, être accrochés les uns aux autres, ou terminés naturellement, ils ne donnent point une marche rapide à l'action, s'ils n'ont pas le mérite de la variété, c'est-à-dire, s'ils ne sont alternativement heureux et malheureux. Voyez *l'Etourdi* de *Moliere*. Nous avons déja dit que cette piece étoit une des plus médiocres de l'Auteur; cependant elle attache. Pourquoi cela? parceque le spectateur est continuellement balloté par des événements qui se contrarient sans cesse, qui l'éloignent de la conclusion quand il croit y toucher, ou qui l'en rapprochent tout-à-coup quand il pense en être bien loin.[97]

The *Dictionnaire dramatique* of 1776, a compendium of everything previously written on the subject of dramatic art, faithfully reproduces whole passages from Diderot without acknowledging the source of information. The authors are particularly attracted to Diderot's suggestions regarding the mechanics of play-construction and like Diderot address the poet thus: "Soit que vous travail-

---

[91] Vol. 8, partie II, article, *Comédie,* by Sulzer, p. 571.
[92] *De l'Art du Théâtre,* 1769, p. 244.
[93] *Du Théâtre, ou Nouvel essai sur l'art dramatique,* 1773, pp. 106–107.
[94] *Op. cit.,* pp. 189–190.   [95] *Mercure de France,* mars 1768, p. 196.
[96] Vol. II, pp. 388–397.   [97] Vol. I, p. 170.

liez sur un sujet connu, soit que vous en tentiez un nouveau, commencez par esquisser la fable . . ."[98] And the authors do not overlook the paragraph of Diderot which begins "Le plan d'un drame
peut être fait et bien fait, sans que le poëte sache rien encore du
caractere qu'il attachera à ses personnages."[99]

La Harpe writes of Sedaine and *le Philosophe sans le savoir*:
". . . il prodigue dans sa pièce, d'après le système de Diderot, tous
ces petits accessoires indifférens qui ne servent qu'à remplir les
scènes d'inutilités. Mais un art particulier à Sedaine, c'est de tirer
quelquefois des effets de ces mots qui semblent ne rien signifier."[100]
Although La Harpe does not approve of the method suggested by
Diderot, it is interesting to note that he was aware of it and that he
perceived an analogy between it and the practice of Sedaine.

The following words of Marmontel sound strangely familiar:
"L'intérêt du poëte, en effet, n'est pas, dans le comique, de tenir le
spectateur en peine, mais bien les personnages: car il s'agit de di-
vertir les témoins aux dépens des acteurs . . ."[101]

The *Annales dramatiques* of 1808, like the *Dictionnaire dramatique* of 1772, pillage Diderot whenever necessary. For example,
Diderot had written: "Le premier acte d'un drame en est peut-être
la portion la plus difficile. Il faut qu'il entame, qu'il marche, quelquefois qu'il expose, et toujours qu'il lie." The sentences reoccur
with slight variation: "Le premier acte d'un drame est peut-être le
plus difficile. Il faut qu'il entame, qu'il marche, qu'il développe les
caractères, qu'il expose le sujet, et surtout qu'il lie l'action."[102]

Directly or indirectly, then, Diderot's ideas on dramatic structure seem to have filtered through the end of the eighteenth century
to the first part of the nineteenth century.[103] Obviously, this influ-

---

[98] Vol. II, pp. 433–434. Cf. Diderot, *De la Poésie dramatique*, pp. 322–323.
[99] *Ibid.*, pp. 435–436. Cf. Diderot, *op. cit.*, p. 347.
[100] *Correspondance littéraire*, 1801, vol. I, Lettre V, 1774, p. 48.
[101] *Oeuvres complettes*, 1787, v. 5, *Elémens de littérature*, tome premier,
article, *Action,* pp. 55–56.
[102] Vol. I, article, *Acte,* p. 77.
[103] One might note also their penetration through to the present day.
Thanks to Lessing's indebtedness to Diderot and thanks to a curious error of
Professor George Baker, Diderot's discussion on surprise and suspense
figures in Professor Baker's recent manual on dramatic technique. Professor Baker quotes the words as belonging to Lessing without observing that
they were taken from Diderot. (Baker, George, *Dramatic Technique*, 1919,
pp. 212–213.)

ence would have been impossible without the work of his predecessors; it was so immediate and so effective only because he codified the aspirations of his contemporaries. While there appears to be little doubt about the fact of Diderot's influence, in a certain sense the beneficence of the influence he exerted may be questionable. Unfortunately, we have with Diderot the beginning of the simplification and restriction of the art of the drama to the science of playwriting. What constitutes for Diderot the elements of a successful play? Listen to him: "Si le plan de l'ouvrage est bien fait, si le poëte a bien choisi son premier moment, s'il est entré par le centre de l'action, s'il a bien dessiné ses caractères, comment n'aurait-il pas du succès?" And we must not forget that, lest the clause on the portrayal of characters be misunderstood, he hastens to qualify it by adding the final reserve, ". . . c'est aux situations à décider des caractères."[104] Provided the plot has been well planned, provided it has been well developed, provided it has been brought to a logical *dénouement,* it is inconceivable to Diderot that the play could be unsuccessful. This mechanical criterion for judging a play was pleasing to the majority of Diderot's contemporaries. It will be interesting to see later to what extent they adopted it, enlarged upon it, and made it their own.

We observe, in conclusion, that modern critics have invariably noted Diderot's conscious effort to rehabilitate *le naturel* in eighteenth century French drama. They might have noted, too, that, consciously or unconsciously, it was Diderot who helped impose upon the dramatic productions of the next fifty or sixty years conventions no less artificial than the ones which he set out to destroy.

In spite of scattered attempts, like those of Palissot in *les Tuteurs,* to revive an ancient *genre,* in spite of excellent indications given by a critic like Fréron, joyful comedy steadily ceased to attract the best efforts of contemporary authors. In 1756 Grimm writes that Seillans' *Gageure de village,* a play after the manner of Dancourt, only serves to renew "nos regrets d'avoir vu la gaieté se retirer de notre scène et faire place à l'esprit toujours si froid et si triste."[105] The situation has not improved three years later for La

[104] *De la Poésie dramatique,* p. 347.
[105] *Correspondance littéraire,* v. 3, 1er juin 1756, p. 231.

Porte is witness to the fact that in 1759 "Une comédie nouvelle, bien reçue du Public, est aujourd'hui une sorte de phénomène. Les tentatives, dans ce genre, sont très-rares, et les succès encore moins fréquens."[106] In spite of the perceptible advances which had been made in securing recognition for the value of plot, the plot of comedy had not been cultivated in sufficient measure to satisfy contemporary critics or there would have been no cause for the following complaint by a critic of the *Mercure:*

> L'action théâtrale, j'ose le dire, est plus vive dans les bonnes Tragédies modernes, qu'elle ne l'a jamais été; et si elles sont moins satisfaisantes à la lecture, elles sont plus animées et plus frappantes au Théâtre . . .
>
> . . . Ce que la Tragédie a acquis du côté de l'action, la Comédie l'a perdu, et le *Médisant* en est un exemple. Les détails et le caractere principal de cette Piece sont dignes de l'Auteur du *Glorieux;* mais elle manque d'intrigue, de tableaux, de situations enfin, sans lesquelles point de vrai comique.[107]

There is no doubt about the shift in emphasis and the demand for a substantial, well-developed plot. La Porte's criticisms in 1759 of contemporary and earlier dramatists are a certain indication of this fact. Although he does not refuse, for example, to accord Boissy "un esprit brillant, une imagination vive, une versification légere, un coloris gracieux, un talent rare pour le Dialogue, et une connoissance parfaite des ridicules du siécle," he regrets that "on ne trouve pas toujours dans ses Comédies un plan bien imaginé, ni une intrigue bien conduite. Il sçavoit composer une scène, et non une Pièce entiere . . ."[108] Likewise, Gresset's proficiency in his contrast of characters and the variety of his portraits in the *Méchant* do not excuse the lack of action in the play. While La Porte thinks that "il seroit difficile à M. *Gresset* de mal versifier," he finds that "Il n'en est pas toujours ainsi du plan d'une Piéce de Théâtre, de la marche, de l'effet qu'elle doit produire, du choix du sujet et des caractères; en un mot, de ce qui constitue le Poëme dramatique en général; car dans cette partie M. *Gresset* me paroît n'avoir réussi que médiocrement."[109]

[106] *L'Observateur, littéraire,* v. 4, 1759, pp. 162–163.
[107] *Mercure de France,* décembre 1758, pp. 188–189.
[108] *Op. cit.,* v. 1, 1759, p. 235.   [109] *Op. cit.,* v. 2, pp. 158–160, *passim.*

On the contrary, what does La Porte admire in Regnard? "Il conduit bien une intrigue, expose clairement le sujet; le noeud se forme sans contrainte; l'action prend une marche réguliere; chaque incident lui donne un nouveau degré de chaleur; l'intérêt croît jusquà (*sic*) un dénouement heureux, tiré du fonds même de la Piéce."[110] Dufresny has ceased to be popular with the critic because "presque toutes ses Comédies offrent plus d'invention, que de conduite; des plans peu réguliers, des dénouemens trop brusqués."[111] While he admits in regard to Hauteroche that "il ne faut pas chercher dans cet Auteur, ni détails ni moeurs, ni aucun de ces caractères propres à les corriger," he is enthusiastic over a "plan sagement construit, soutenu par une marche réguliere; une intrigue bien conduite, agréablement dialoguée; des scènes coupées avec art, variées par divers incidens; un dénouement heureux, pour l'ordinaire . . ." He delights, too, in Hauteroche's valets. And why?—because, "il se plaît à multiplier leurs embarras, à les jetter dans des labyrinthes d'où ils semblent ne devoir jamais sortir, pour les en tirer adroitement, lorsque tout paroît désespéré. La surprise alors est aussi agréable, que le noeud de l'intrigue avoit causé d'inquiétude."[112]

For the moment, however, the eighteenth century's principal interest in the theater is centered elsewhere than in comedy. The possibilities of a new *genre* enticingly beckon to authors at the beginning of a road as yet relatively untried. A rabid philosophical spirit, too, is on the point of invading the theater to the exclusion of all other considerations. When the reaction comes, as it inevitably will, when the interest of the century again turns to the old and temporarily abandoned *genre,* the newly formulated principles will not be overlooked. Indeed, it is inconceivable that comedy will fail to find renewed inspiration in the principles of a *poétique* which coincides so closely with its own latent tendencies.

---

[110] *Op. cit.,* v. 4, p. 155. It is interesting to note that, at the beginning of the century, Regnard, Dufresny, and Dancourt had, generally speaking, been equally successful writers. Because of his special skill in constructing a good *comédie d'intrigue*, Regnard is the one whose work increases in importance with the passing decades. Critics begin to see in his comedies things which had not been fully appreciated before.

[111] *Op. cit.,* v. 2, 1760, p. 24.   [112] *Ibid.,* pp. 227–228.

CHAPTER IV

1760–1775

Revival of interest in comedy with a frankly gay tone and in the *comédie d'intrigue;* Goldoni.—Bret, Rochon de Chabannes, Barthe, Sedaine, Cailhava and the *comédie d'intrigue.*—Theories of Beaumarchais concerning plot and its construction.—Evidences of the new attitude toward good plot-construction.

The philosophical spirit which invaded the theater about 1760 was of relatively short duration; one can safely ascribe its reign in the field of comedy to the years between 1760 and 1765.[1] While the dominant concern of the century with "le philosophe" submerged for the time being its minor but no less real interest in plot, it in no wise entirely obscured it. Indeed, one of the chief criticisms of comedies such as Voltaire's *l'Ecossaise* and Palissot's *les Philosophes* is that their authors have neglected what had come to be considered one of the chief requisites of a comic play. Fréron qualifies the former play as "une prétendue Comédie, où il n'y a ni vraisemblance, ni liaison, ni intérêt, ni marche, ni chaleur, ni action . . ."[2] An anonymous critic asks the author of *les Philosophes,* "Qu'est-ce que votre intrigue? c'est un noeud qui est si imperceptible qu'on ne peut le voir qu'avec vos yeux; il n'est fondé sur rien, si on excepte les injures qui remplissent chaque Scène."[3] Grimm marvels at the tumult caused by such a play since "On n'y trouve ni plan, ni intrigue, ni conduite, ni caractère, ni plaisanterie,

---

[1] The following table, drawn from Ira O. Wade's enumeration of eighteenth century comedies in which "le philosophe" as he was known in life is portrayed, is indicative of the trend of the time:

Years	Number of plays
1740–1745	1
1746–1749	1
1750–1754	2
1755–1759	2
1760–1765	18
1766–1769	2
1770–1775	4

(*The "Philosophe" in the French Drama of the Eighteenth Century.*)

[2] *L'Année littéraire,* 1760, v. 5, p. 285.

[3] *Les Qu'est-ce? A l'auteur de la comédie des Philosophes,* 1760, p. 27.

ni force, ni légèreté, ni rien de ce qu'on est en droit d'exiger d'une pièce de théâtre."[4]

That these criticisms represent the prevailing consensus of contemporary opinion is evidenced by the reaction of Lamarche-Courmont who feels called upon to defend Palissot. His apology is very significant; in virtue of the fact that it is written from a negative point of view, one must conclude that it is a reply to a positive demand. Our author admits that he does not wish to exclude amorous plots or *comédies d'intrigue* but he adds that the latter

> sont les seules où l'on doive rechercher l'intrigue pour elle-même : il suffit dans une Piéce de caractére que les Scenes soient amenées et dessinées. On ne demande dans ces sortes de Piéces que des tableaux vrais et peints avec goût ; elles n'ont besoin, ni de noeuds, ni de dénouemens frappans, ni en un mot de toute cette petite magie qui ne pique que la curiosité, et que l'esprit dédaigne . . .[5]

In spite of the ridiculous light in which "le philosophe" was often presented in contemporary plays, any comedy which treats this character must be inspired by a certain basic seriousness. Now the eighteenth century enjoyed being serious and especially at the Comédie-Française. This had been more or less true ever since the advent of Destouches. In 1761 Sablier declares[6] that Melpomene continues to triumph over Thalia and that it is no longer in the best taste to witness the performance of a good, old-fashioned comedy. The following year Grimm prophesies[7] that it will soon be impossible to be frankly comic except at the Théâtres de la Foire—a prophecy which proved to be only too true. From 1760 on, however, one can trace a growing reaction to this state of mind and a definite interest in any manifestation of the comic spirit.

One of the most obvious indications of this reaction is the critic's praise of authors who attempt to revive the ancient comic *genre*. The *Mercure de France* of 1761 welcomes Belcourt's *les Fausses Apparences,* "d'un genre qui demande que l'on encourage ceux qui font des efforts pour le rétablir sur notre Théâtre. L'intrigue de cette Piéce est construite avec art ; elle produit les situations ; et les

---

[4] *Correspondance littéraire,* v. 4, juin 1760, p. 239.
[5] *Réponse aux différens écrits publiés contre la comédie des Philosophes,* 1760, p. 60.
[6] *Oeuvres de M***,* 1761, p. 20.   [7] *Op. cit.,* v. 5, février 1762, p. 43.

situations servent à soutenir l'intrigue, en en renouvellant l'*imbro-glio,* dont l'obscurité n'existe que pour les Acteurs."[8] *L'Avant-cou-reur* sees in Bret's *l'Epreuve indiscrette* "la louable envie de nous rappeller à l'ancien genre qui n'est que trop oublié de nos jours."[9] The *Mercure de France* is of the opinion that one should be grate-ful to Barthe "d'avoir ramené le rire qui sembloit nous être interdit . . . et l'on ne sauroit trop l'engager à poursuivre une carrière où ses premiers pas ont été si heureux."[10] In like spirit, Rochon de Chabannes' *Valets maîtres de la maison* is greeted as "une pièce du genre de celles qui, dans ce temps, faisoient rire nos pères ; . . . le succès qu'elle continue d'avoir, justifie son idée."[11] And the fol-lowing year, "On a sçu gré à M. Cailhava d'avoir ramené sur notre théâtre l'ancienne gaïté, qui est peut-être trop négligée au-jourd'hui . . ."[12] Fréron goes so far as to judge Cailhava's *Mariage interrompu* less harshly than he might otherwise have done, for "la Pièce est gaie, et c'est un mérite si rare aujourd'hui qu'on peut en sa faveur lui pardonner bien des défauts."[13] In 1772 Aubert considers that there is in *la Mère jalouse* of Barthe "de l'excellent comique, du comique de Molière. Qu'il n'ait pas été goûté autant qu'il méritoit de l'être, nous n'en sommes pas surpris : ce genre est aujourd'hui hors de mode. Mais on ne sauroit trop s'efforcer d'y ramener le public ; et c'est en cela que M. Barthe mérite l'éloge de tous les gens sensés . . ."[14]

If attempts like those of Barthe had been at all satisfactory, they would probably have received no little applause, for contemporary writings reflect a favorable attitude on the part of the public toward comic plays. The *Mercure de France* notes in connection with Cailhava's second *comédie d'intrigue,* "il paroît avoir voulu sonder le goût actuel du Public pour l'ancienne comédie, et s'as-surer, par son expérience, qu'on la verroit encore avec plaisir ; ses succès doivent l'encourager à tenter de nouveaux essors et à traiter des caracteres."[15] Bachaumont recounts a curious incident which, although it may have had no direct influence on Beaumarchais, is

---

[8] Septembre 1761, p. 211.   [9] 1764, p. 108.
[10] Mars 1768, p. 188.
[11] *Mercure de France,* mars 1768, pp. 200–201.
[12] *Op. cit.,* mai 1769, p. 143.   [13] *Op. cit.,* 1769, v. 3, p. 189.
[14] *Journal des beaux-arts et des sciences,* v. 1, mars 1772, p. 474.
[15] Mai 1769, p. 144.

not without significance. Preparations were being made in 1769 for the dramatic representations at Versailles and His Majesty had drawn up the list of plays which were to be given.

> Elle a rayé de sa main le *Philosophe sans le sçavoir, Eugenie* et *Beverley,* par la raison que ces drames tristes et lugubres ne convenoient point à son âge, qui n'avoit besoin que de choses agréables et gaies. Les Sieurs *Sedaine, Caron de Beaumarchais* et *Saurin* sont très-affligés de cette disgrace, et sans doute vont échauffer leur imagination pour enfanter des comédies plus comiques, et plus propres à plaire à leur Souverain.[16]

In 1773, Grimm, although he cannot conceal his dislike for Cailhava's *Tuteur dupé* or for the *genre* it represents, admits, "Le succès de cette pièce telle quelle, du plus mauvais genre, si vous le voulez, prouve toujours que notre parterre serait encore fort disposé à rire, si la plupart de nos auteurs n'avaient pas trop d'esprit ou trop de sensibilité dans l'âme pour être gais et plaisants."[17]

These various bits of evidence lead one to conclude that the eighteenth century was beginning to feel the need for comedy with a frankly gayer tone. As everyone knows, the kind of play which was eventually adopted to satisfy the need was the gay *comédie d'intrigue* of Beaumarchais. What are some of the reasons which led to a revival of this *genre?*

Obviously, it is impossible to ignore the work of the preceding sixty years. A change in attitude which had developed so slowly, so steadily and ingrained itself so deeply in the thought of the century cannot be lightly brushed aside. The average critic at the beginning of the century—Lesage was the exception—would not have said, as Fréron did in 1761 of a play of Riccoboni, "Cette pièce a les deux premières qualités du comique; elle est très-bien intriguée et pleine de gaîté."[18] Nor would he have said with the critic of *le Censeur hebdomadaire* in regard to *l'Epouse à la mode* of La Place, "Cette Pièce est bien écrite. Que lui a-t-il manqué pour réussir? Plus d'action."[19]

Plot had become an integral part of the *comédie de caractère* and was considered by the majority of critics as essential as the

---

[16] *Mémoires secrets,* etc., v. 19, 1783, additions, p. 109, 30 juin 1769.
[17] *Op. cit.,* v. 10, avril 1773, p. 222.   [18] *Op. cit.,* 1761, v. 7, p. 270.
[19] 1760, v. 5. Table des Matières, Article IX.

characters. Diderot carried the evolution a step further when he subordinated the characters of a play to the construction of the plot. During the years immediately preceding and succeeding the publication of *De la Poésie dramatique,* interest in the *drame* had diverted attention from comedy. With a revival of interest in the latter, and especially in real comedy, the movement already begun in this *genre* continues its course, reinforced by the sanction and prestige of Diderot and by an increased consciousness of its own earlier, but more timidly formulated standards. One should not imagine that we are wholly attributing the revival of the *comédie d'intrigue* to Diderot's theoretical treatises—nothing could be further from the truth. We have seen that, long before Diderot,. comedy had started on this new path. And yet, it seems obvious that Diderot greatly accelerated the movement by gathering up scattered ideas and giving them new emphasis. Comedy acquired something from this contact with Diderot, if nothing more than authorization for its own tendencies. Because it could do nothing else at the moment of this contact, it was forced to accept his criteria.

Certain dramatic complexes and dramatic inadequacies concurred to make this result inevitable. As the century advanced, the hopelessness of attempting to rival Molière in the portrayal of character became increasingly evident. The heights to which he had attained and the distance which separated him from his less successful imitators seem to have paralyzed the efforts of eighteenth century dramatists and to have discouraged them from making similar attempts. Beaumarchais at first turned to the *drame* "où l'on peut de nouveau s'emparer avec succès des grands caractères de la Comédie, qui sont à peu-près épuisés sous leur titre propre . . ."[20] Throughout the whole century dramatists labored under the impression, correct or incorrect, that characters suitable for portrayal on the stage had been exhausted and that nothing remained for them to do in this field. That this complex was, to a certain extent, the result of incompetency does not lessen the fact of its existence nor invalidate its influence on the shift in dramatic emphasis. If the character element of a play does not attract dramatists' attention, the plot element will.

A similar situation faced the author of the *comédie de moeurs.*

[20] *Essai sur le genre dramatique sérieux,* 1767, p. xxxii.

A clever satire of contemporary manners without a plot to substantiate it was not likely to be acclaimed by critics as a comedy worthy of the name. In connection with a review of *les Moeurs du tems,* the *Mercure de France* undertakes an apology of the *comédie de moeurs* without plot. This particular play had been much applauded, but the plot was very simple, "ce qui a donné lieu à quelques critiques de la juger foible . . ."[21] The critic maintains, however, that it would probably have been less successful had the plot been stronger. Since the main object of this comedy was to paint various aspects of social customs open to ridicule, such a canvas would have been obscured by a more complicated action. It may be true that in some plays of like nature a substantial plot is an advantage. If critics will remember that, fundamentally, "la Comédie ne doit être qu'une imitation naïve des moeurs et des actions privées de la société,"[22] they will not demand that its very essence be subordinated to any other aspect of dramatic art. In spite of this apology, however, Grimm continues to apply the newer criterion to the *comédie de moeurs.* Poinsinet's *le Cercle ou la Soirée à la mode,* for example, had been successful and while Grimm admits that it presented a fairly striking picture of contemporary Parisian society, he maintains, "Ce n'est point là une comédie: il n'a point d'intrigue, point de scènes, et surtout point de dialogue . . ."[23]

Certain social changes reinforced this tendency to emphasize plot and rendered impotent any attempts to prolong the classical *comédie de moeurs* and more especially the *comédie de caractère.* Modern critics[24] have attributed the cultivation of *comédie de caractère* in the seventeenth century and its lack of cultivation in the nineteenth to the fact that the various social classes were more distinct in the seventeenth century than after the Revolution. The subsequent mingling of classes tended to efface distinguishing characteristics and to foster uniformity. This breaking down of social hierarchies, begun in the eighteenth century, did not have its full effect on the theater until the nineteenth century. It would be idle to suppose, however, that the causes which resulted in an ultimate dissolution had no influence upon the eighteenth century theater. With a

---

[21] Février 1761, p. 197.   [22] *Ibid.,* pp. 198–199.
[23] *Op. cit.,* v. 6, 15 septembre 1764, p. 69.
[24] Parigot, *Emile Augier,* 1890, p. 109 f.

long perspective, it is not difficult for the modern critic to determine the progress and effects of this evolution. An eighteenth century writer like Linguet, who was aware of what was happening, shows his critical acumen.

In 1774, with discouragement and resignation, Linguet attributes the dearth of good comedies to changes in the social structure.[25] Universal corruption has insinuated itself into every social stratum because of the confusion of classes. People are more polished and more depraved; they have few faults, only vices which are easily concealed under a mask of uniformity. Every man has the same appearance and seems to have had the same training. In consequence, ridicule is no longer possible and comedy's legitimate inspiration ceases to function. The uniformity of contemporary manners would make the dramatic picture colorless should the artist attempt a faithful reproduction of external appearances; the corruption at the basis of these same manners would make the dramatic picture cruel, should the artist attempt a true reproduction of underlying aims and motives. That in itself, according to Linguet, is sufficient cause for alarm, but that is not all:

> si la vraie *Comédie* essaie quelquefois de s'égayer encore sur des travers innocens, si elle tâche de saisir quelques nuances adoucies qui la rapprochent un peu de ses anciens succès, elle se trouve à chaque pas accablée d'entraves et dégoûtée par des obstacles. Chaque corps, chaque état devient plus délicat en raison de ce que la caducité politique et morale devient plus universelle et plus sensible. Plus les abus se multiplient, plus on redoute la main qui les dévoileroit.

A similar condition results from certain misalliances engendered by the mania of the "bourgeois" to ally himself with the nobility. Such follies furnished Molière and his immediate successors with some excellent comic turns; "elle ne nous feroit plus rire. Il n'est plus ridicule qu'un Roturier riche fasse d'un Noble pauvre son frère, son gendre ou son cousin. La nation est toute entière fondée sur ces alliances, et elle ne s'amuseroit pas d'une satyre qui attaqueroit un défaut incorporé dans ses moeurs."

From this visible change in the social structure it follows, then,

---

[25] *Journal de politique et de littérature,* v. 1, 1774. For the following discussion compare pp. 100–105, *passim.*

that comedy no longer has at its command resources which it once enjoyed. It can only become finer, more polished, more monotonous, more tiresome. Even as the conversations which it seeks to reproduce, it must take on a tinge of metaphysics and a smack of philosophy in order to gloss over with pretty words its own vaporousness. And Linguet concludes disconsolately:

C'est aussi ce qui arrive: regretter cette décadence, c'est perdre son tems; en chercher le remède, c'est le perdre encore davantage; tel est le sort des choses humaines. On naît, on s'accroît, on existe un moment, on dégénère, et enfin on périt, jusqu'à ce que l'on soit ranimé en tout ou en partie sous d'autres formes . . .

The rebirth of comedy in a new form was about to take place, sooner, perhaps, than our critic anticipated. That authors had begun to concentrate more exclusively than ever on plot, the one element of dramatic art still perfectible, is attested to by Nougaret in 1769. Nougaret observes that with the Ancients the plot of a play was usually simple. "Depuis quelques années nous commençons à nous écarter des Anciens, nos Drames sont surchargés d'intrigue, de merveilleux, de situations forcées."[26] A similar observation on the part of Linguet corroborates the statement of Nougaret and indicates that the latter has not exaggerated. Authors can no longer confine themselves to the simplicity which furnished their predecessors with so many masterpieces. "Il faut aujourd'hui de grands mouvemens sur la scène. Il faut des actions intriguées; on cherche à affecter les yeux et l'esprit, plus encore que le coeur."[27] And Linguet, quite in keeping with the spirit of his time, concludes later that *les Femmes savantes* "comme toutes les comédies de ce créateur du théatre chez nous sont vuides d'intrigue et même d'intérêt."[28]

On the whole, far from protesting against this tendency, critics encourage it either directly or indirectly. The *Mercure de France*, for example, notes that Desnon's *Julie* is extremely simple but that the author extracted everything possible from the *conte* which served as source. While the author is urged to continue his career,

[26] *Op. cit.*, pp. 190–191, *passim*.
[27] *Théâtre espagnol*, 1770, Avertissement, v. 1, p. xiv.
[28] *Ibid.*, v. 3, *On ne badine pas avec l'amour*, Avertissement.

the critic exhorts him "à ne pas négliger l'action; son premier essai n'en offre peut-être pas assez."[29] In connection with Barthe's *l'Homme personnel,* La Harpe admits, "le défaut d'intrigue et le vide d'action sont des maladies mortelles. Quoi de plus froid que le noeud de cette pièce!"[30] Elsewhere, in regard to the 1778 edition of Saint Foix, he says, *"L'Oracle et les Grâces* se recommandent par la délicatesse des idées, et par des tableaux rians et voluptueux, quoique ce genre de féerie et de mythologie soit très-inférieur, non seulement au comique de caractère, mais aux moindres petites pièces où il y a de la gaîté et de l'intrigue."[31] The *Journal de politique et de littérature* says of *Henri IV ou la Bataille d'Ivry,* "Il est impossible de rendre compte du plan, de l'intrigue, ou même du fonds de cette pièce: elle n'en a point . . . L'Auteur semble ne s'être point du tout proposé de faire une pièce: il n'a voulu que construire un cadre où il pût enchâsser . . . une partie des *mots* attribués à *Henri IV* . . ."[32]

It is evident from the preceding examples that for the average critic plot has become of such importance that it must be present in almost any kind of comedy. The public, too, had its share, perhaps the greater share, in determining the kind of comedy which it was willing to witness and applaud. Bachaumont remarks that the public had been more enthusiastic than usual over the ordinarily dull author of *les Fausses infidélités.* The reason, in addition to excellent acting, is this: "On a trouvé dans son drame une adresse d'intrigue, une vivacité de dialogue, un piquant de style, qui lui a procuré tous les souffrages."[33] Several years later, in connection with a review of Palissot's *les Courtisannes ou l'Ecole des moeurs,* Linguet agrees that the author might justify the extreme simplicity of his play on the grounds that the object of comedy has always been to portray the foibles and vices of the time and that if nothing is lacking in the truth of this picture, one can scarcely demand anything more. Theoretically, this is all very true; actually,

Le plus grand nombre des Lecteurs, il faut en convenir, trouvera cette intrigue trop simple, trop nue, trop peu travaillée. L'Auteur aura beau

[29] Juillet 1769, v. 2, p. 177.
[30] *Correspondance littéraire,* 1801, v. 2, Lettre LXXXIII (n. d.), p. 210.
[31] *Ibid.,* Lettre LXXX (n. d.), p. 194.
[32] *Op. cit.,* v. 1, p. 137.   [33] *Op. cit.,* v. 3, p. 318.

répondre qu'il ne pouvoit donner à sa Pièce plus d'action, sans tomber dans l'indécence. Les excuses les plus ingénieuses ne trouveront pas grace, sur ce point, aux yeux du Public, accoutumé, sur-tout depuis quelque tems, à des intrigues plus soutenues et plus compliquées.[34]

This urgent demand on the part of critics and public for the dramatist to concentrate on the plot element of comedy was undoubtedly precipitated by the arrival in Paris during the early part of this period of the Italian dramatist, Goldoni. He furnished the concrete example of the ideal toward which the century was converging. That the Italians were past masters in the art of intrigue had long been known to the French public. The arrival of Goldoni at this particular time is of especial significance for he brought to the French theater what it was already predisposed to accept. The eager anticipation which preceded Goldoni's arrival, the enthusiasm with which he was greeted, and the praise which he received are ample proof of this fact.

In August 1761, the *Mercure de France* remarks simply, "Quelques Amateurs desireroient que notre Scène profitât de l'attention avec laquelle le célèbre M. *Goldoni* recherche les traces des Comiques de l'Antiquité."[35] In September of the same year the *Mercure* announces[36] that according to the latest rumour arrangements are being made to bring Goldoni to Paris and to engage him in the task of rejuvenating the Théâtre Italien. It is the fervent hope of the *Mercure* that this project will be realized, for Goldoni's presence would lead to emulation and encouragement for the French stage, too.

Most French critics are quick to appreciate Goldoni's talent. *L'Avant-coureur* says everyone knows "avec quel art admirable M. Goldoni sçait rassembler une foule d'incidents, les faire naître l'un de l'autre, les croiser, les développer, les entasser même sans surcharger son sujet, et sans s'accrocher à des épisodes hors d'oeuvre et inutiles, comme dans la plûpart des drames du jour où les scènes de remplissage font presque toute la pièce."[37] Grimm observes that the Italians in general and Goldoni in particular excel especially in what they call *imbroglio;* their plays are masterpieces in this *genre.*

---

[34] *Op. cit.*, v. 1, 1775, pp. 469–470.
[36] Pp. 212–213.

[35] P. 173.
[37] 1763, pp. 669–670.

And he concedes good-naturedly; "Ce n'est pas là la bonne comédie; elle n'a ni caractères ni moeurs; mais lorsqu'on a donné toute la journée aux occupations et aux affaires, elle est bien propre à amuser et à délasser le soir."[38] The following year, although he has not changed his mind about the inferiority of the *genre,* he evidences enthusiastic admiration and keen appreciation for the peculiar talent of Goldoni:

> . . . il entende l'imbroglio supérieurement. Donnez-lui une clef, un portrait, une corbeille; il ne lui en faut pas davantage pour faire une pièce qui vous amusera depuis le commencement jusqu'à la fin. Il tirera un parti infini du plus petit accident avec une adresse merveilleuse; il préparera des riens, et s'en servira un moment après avec un grand avantage et une extrême finesse.[39]

Two or three decades earlier Goldoni might not have been justly appreciated. At this particular moment not only was his talent admired by critics, but his success inspired contemporary authors to cultivate the same *genre.*

Favart, for example, recognizes that there is no modern dramatist who understands the theater better than Goldoni although he reproaches him for neglecting some of its "rules." He is dubious about the ultimate value of Italian comedy because it speaks only to the eye with its rapid movement, complicated plot, and variety in stage decoration. However that may be, Favart finds it correct to admit that "Goldoni, malgré ses irrégularités, sert aujourd'hui de modèle à nos auteurs comiques français . . ."[40] Likewise, Fréron observes that the plays of Goldoni are a new mine for French dramatists. They have exhausted the resources offered by the English and are now resorting to the Italians.[41] Finally, Goldoni himself tells us in his *Mémoires* that since his arrival in France, not a year has passed without a French writer's requesting permission to translate his plays into French for production on the French stage. The translator must have had a certain amount of confidence in the fruitfulness of such an enterprise for he was quite willing to

---

[38] *Op. cit.,* v. 6, 1er septembre 1764, p. 65.
[39] *Op. cit.,* v. 6, 1er octobre 1765, pp. 385–386.
[40] *Mémoires et correspondance littéraires, dramatiques et anecdotiques,* 1808, v. 2, 1762, p. 48.
[41] *Op. cit.,* 1761, v. 7, p. 256.

share with Goldoni whatever material profits the venture might bring him.[42]

We see, then, that the accumulation of certain preconceived dramatic notions, persistent mutations in the social structure of France, and an urgent demand for plot on the part of critics and public accompanied by Goldoni's concrete example of what one might expect to accomplish concurred to produce a revival of interest in the *comédie d'intrigue* and furnished contemporary French dramatists with an incentive to cultivate the plot of comedy for its own sake.

In the decade preceding the representation of *le Barbier de Séville,* there are specific, although not very successful, attempts to revive the ancient *genre.* When evaluating the work of this decade, one cannot overemphasize the seriousness of the situation in which dramatists found themselves. Ever since the *comédie larmoyante* and the *drame* had invaded the theater, real comedy had been relegated to other places and to other interests. Because they were still dominated by the ancient classification, dramatists who had begun their careers in the decade or two preceding 1765 were somewhat dubious about the relative value which should be assigned to the various comic *genres.* On the other hand, their attempts to continue the classical *comédie de caractère* and *comédie de moeurs* not meeting with the desired success, they realized, when it was too late, that new conditions had arisen to make their attempts futile. Bret, who had been writing plays for twenty years, gives an inkling of the situation in the 1765 edition of his plays. When he wrote *la Double extravagance* (1750), he was too young to know the world and impregnated with reminiscences of the ancient theater. Therefore he confined himself to comedy based on a combination of incidents rather than on a study of character and manners. Since these youthful efforts, he has tried to study men more closely and to produce something more profound, "mais les vices qui lui restoient à appercevoir, intéressoient si fort l'humanité, et par conséquent passoient de si loin le ridicule, qu'il a regretté plus d'une fois un genre qu'un peu plus de maturité dans l'esprit, lui avoit fait

[42] *Mémoires,* 1787, v. 3, p. 74.

abandonner."[43] The criticism evoked by his *Epreuve indiscrette* indicates that a more successful reversion to his early practice would be rather welcome, for *l'Avant-coureur* sees in the play "indépendamment de l'esprit et de la connoissance du théâtre, la louable envie de nous rappeller à l'ancien genre qui n'est que trop oublié de nos jours."[44]

The new generation of writers was less hampered than the old by the traditional hierarchy of comic *genres* and more willing to perceive the changing tastes of a new order. Rochon de Chabannes, who in 1762 had successfully tried his skill in a *comédie d'intrigue, Heureusement,* continues the same *genre* in 1768 with his *Valets maîtres de la maison.* The author tells us that although he had not hoped for the favor of contemporary critics, they were very generous to him. "What!" ask people who pride themselves on having good taste, "a farce in this age and at the Théâtre-Français!" "And why not?" replies Rochon de Chabannes, "Molière, Regnard, and Le Sage wrote farces. Why should you take me to task because I want to amuse you?"[45]

Les Fausses infidélités (1768) of Barthe may be considered another manifestation of the contemporary dramatist's interest in the *comédie d'intrigue.* Critical opinion was divided as to its merits but the general public welcomed it with pleasure and during the year 1768 it was given twenty-eight times, no small number for an eighteenth century play.[46]

The most valiant efforts to restore the *genre* were made by Cailhava. One can trace a very decided development in Cailhava's attitude toward the value which should be assigned to plot.[47] He began his career with the production of *la Présomption à la mode,* a five-act *comédie de caractère.* Cailhava's friends attributed the play's lack of success to the fact that it was "dans l'ancien genre." Dissatisfied with this explanation, Cailhava undertook a second play from which he deliberately planned to exclude those traits which seemed to attract public favor such as maxims, pure love

[43] *Oeuvres de théâtre,* 1765, *la Double extravagance,* Avertissement.
[44] 1764, p. 108.
[45] *Les Valets maîtres de la maison,* 1769, Préface, pp. iii–iv.
[46] Cf. Joannidès, *op. cit.*
[47] For the following discussion, cf. *le Mariage interrompu,* 1769, Préface, *passim.*

scenes, bantering, play on words, tearful scenes, etc. The indulgence with which the public greeted this play, *le Tuteur dupé,* soon made him forget the difficulties which he had encountered in having it played. The success of this comedy encouraged him to write another of the same type which was also favorably received by the public. The reason for its success, if Cailhava can trust his friends, is that the public approved his resolution not to abandon "l'ancien genre." Strange to say, however, some of his admirers were a bit disappointed not to find in this latest play, *le Mariage interrompu,* any notable portrayal of character. According to Cailhava, the public considers him capable of working in a more serious *genre* now that it finds him "assez initié dans l'Art si difficile d'exposer, d'intriguer, de dénouer des Scenes et des Actes, de les écrire et de les varier, de les tirer sur-tout du fond d'un Sujet . . ."[48]

Cailhava's own experience, and not his acquaintance with the old masters, taught him that a carefully combined, substantial plot had become the first requisite of a successful comedy. It is true that he claims to be restoring an ancient *genre;* nevertheless his admiration for Plautus, Terence and Molière should not lead one to the erroneous conclusion that he did not appreciate the gulf which separated the ancients' conception of plot-construction from that which had become current in his own time. The door scene of the *Miles Gloriosus* inspired him to write *le Tuteur dupé.* He expressly states that this device allowed him to obtain various comic tricks and mistaken identities which, in order to create an illusion, necessitated neither the "masque" of the ancients nor "la complaisance outrée des Spectateurs."[49]

He is equally aware that there are defects in the Latin play which a French dramatist must avoid. With Plautus, the false door and the resemblance between the two sisters are not announced until the second act and even then without art. Cailhava tries to fix the attention of the public on these two elements in the very first scene of his play.[50] He agrees, too, with Diderot, that nothing short of the genius of Molière would enable an author to amuse his public now with "une intrigue à la grecque, dont les Marchands d'es-

[48] *Ibid.,* p. v.
[49] *Théâtre,* 1781, v. 1, *le Tuteur dupé,* Préface de l'édition de 1778, p. 201.
[50] *Ibid.,* pp. 201–202.

claves, les filles exposées, vendues et retrouvées, etc., etc. font tout l'intérêt."[51] Elsewhere Cailhava addresses Molière:

> Tu ne marches pas sur les traces de *Plaute,* qui, dans un prologue, instruit le spectateur de tout ce qui doit arriver, et enleve par-là toute espece d'intérêt. Tu ne racontes pas froidement, comme Térence, l'avant-scène à un esclave qui ne doit pas avoir part à l'action . . . Tu devines qu'une exposition doit être courte, rapide, claire; que le Public veut être instruit promptement des événements qui ont précédé une action déjà avancée, du lieu où elle se passera, et ne voir faire confidence qu'à un personnage utile; qu'il désire enfin de tenir dans ses mains, avant la fin du premier acte, les fils de tous les ressorts de la machine, sans deviner les effets qu'ils produiront.[52]

In reviving what he terms "l'ancien genre," Cailhava is aware, then, of the modifications it must undergo in order to be acceptable to his contemporary public. Cailhava's answer to his friends' suggestion that he now try to portray living characters is quite in keeping with what we have already found to be one of the preconceived notions of the century and positive proof that whatever the theoretical ideals of the day may have been, it was practically impossible at this time to reëstablish with success the *comédie de caractère.* Cailhava betrays himself even as he betrays the century:

> Je connais ma faiblesse, je sens combien il est difficile de trouver des Caracteres qui prêtent au vrai Comique, dans un siécle et dans un Pays, où tous les Etats étant confondus par le luxe, où tous les hommes recevant à-peu-pres la même éducation, leurs passions et leurs ridicules, ne peuvent par conséquent offrir qu'un même masque: enfin, je vois en frémissant, l'espace immense que j'ai à franchir; mais je ferai des tentatives qui puissent me rendre digne des encouragemens flatteurs que j'ai reçus.[53]

Contemporary critics do not fail to recognize the spirit animating Cailhava's first dramatic productions and some of them laud what little talent he displays. For example, Bachaumont, on the whole a rather difficult critic to please, says of *le Tuteur dupé,* "L'auteur a l'art de mettre souvent ses personnages dans un em-

[51] *Ibid.,* p. 207.
[52] *Théâtre,* 1781, v. 2, p. 469 (misprint for p. 460). (The reply to an imaginary discourse of Molière on the occasion of his posthumous reception to the French Academy.)
[53] *Le Mariage interrompu,* 1769, Préface, p. v.

barras que partage le spectateur, et pour l'ordinaire les en tire d'une maniere imprévue. On croit que la piece va se dénouer longtems avant le cinquieme acte, une ruse nouvelle remet toujours les choses dans le premier état."[54] Likewise, he finds *le Mariage interrompu* a comedy "dans le vrai ton, amusante, courte, sans épisode, sans tirades, et marchant toujours à l'événement, malgré la complication d'embarras de toute espece, que forme infatigablement le héros de l'intrigue, c'est-à-dire le valet."[55] *L'Avant-coureur* also finds that the play "a du mouvement, de la gaîté, des situations plaisantes et bien amenées. L'intrigue est conduite avec art, elle excite la curiosité, et elle est d'un comique vif qui naît du sujet."[56]

On the other hand, now, as at any other moment of the century, conservative critics oppose the attempt to restore the *comédie d'intrigue*. Fréron admits in 1775, "Il faut qu'une pièce de Théâtre fixe l'attention du Spectateur soit par l'intérêt de l'action, soit par la force de l'intrigue, soit par des caractères frappans."[57] And yet he stubbornly maintains in 1769 that the kind of play which Cailhava practices is no longer in style and cannot make an author's reputation.[58]

Grimm's distaste for the *genre* knows no bounds—theoretically, at any rate. After the representation of *le Tuteur dupé* Grimm admits that the author should be encouraged because he has gayety and a certain ingeniousness, but he adds, "notre goût est si éloigné de ce genre, et ce genre est si éloigné de la bonne comédie!"[59] The *genre* no longer finds a counterpart in real life because valets do not have the same part in their master's affairs which they formerly had. Since it has neither moral truth nor moral aim, since it does not present a true picture of contemporary manners, the *genre* is not worthy of serious consideration and serves only for rest and amusement at the end of the day. He is willing to agree that Cailhava makes one laugh, "qu'il a des saillies assez plaisantes, qu'il noue, dénoue et renoue son intrigue avec assez de facilité." He objects, however, that Cailhava has had to make his *tuteur* excessively stupid in order to assure the success of his valet's tricks.[60]

---

[54] *Op. cit.*, v. 16, p. 262, additions to octobre 1765.
[55] *Op. cit.*, v. 4, 11 avril 1769, p. 256.   [56] 1769, p. 250.
[57] *Op. cit.*, 1775, v. 2, p. 219.   [58] *Op. cit.*, 1769, v. 3, p. 188.
[59] *Op. cit.*, v. 6, octobre 1765, p. 385.   [60] *Ibid.*, p. 388.

When Cailhava again comes before the public with a *comédie-ballet, les Etrennes de l'amour,* Grimm asks, "Et qu'est-ce que M. Cailhava d'Estandoux? C'est un Gascon . . . qui est venu à Paris il y a plusieurs années avec le projet de remettre la comédie farce, la comédie à intrigue en possession du théâtre." The project has not succeeded, according to Grimm; it becomes increasingly difficult to make the French nation laugh for it seems to prefer weeping at the theater. Grimm concludes that Cailhava "paraît du moins avoir abandonné son projet, et il s'est fait marchand d'ambigu, pour avoir quelque chose à offrir au public le jour de l'an."[61]

Cailhava, however, had not abandoned his project and when his *Mariage interrompu* appeared a few months later, Grimm takes up the opposition with more force. "Ce genre de pièce à intrigue où tout roule sur la manigance d'un fripon de valet et sur la duperie des maîtres dont la bêtise est ordinairement hors de toute vraisemblance, ce genre, dis-je, est détestable. Il était bon chez les anciens, il est absurde chez les modernes . . ." His concluding admission is extremely interesting; since the *genre* is hallowed by time, and since men are superstitious, "il y a un certain nombre d'amateurs de théâtre qui prétendent que c'est là la seule et véritable comédie."[62] Such an attitude seems paradoxical when one considers that Grimm's first criticism of plays which are not pure *comédies d'intrigue* is almost invariably, "l'intrigue est faible,"[63] or, "elle est faiblement intriguée."[64] The only explanation for this inconsistency is that comedy without plot is no longer acceptable even to the intelligently conservative critic. He prefers, moreover, to recommend a comedy which combines the advantages of the *comédie d'intrigue* with something he considers a bit deeper. In 1769 the *Mercure de France* encourages Cailhava and exhorts him to enlarge his field so that he will include in his plays the portrayal of characters; the *genre* "dans lequel il s'est essayé jusqu'à présent a son mérite particulier, mais ce n'est pas le grand genre."[65]

And yet, whenever a clever *comédie d'intrigue* came to light, the eighteenth century did not refuse the author merited applause and encouragement, as we have seen, for example, in the case of Gol-

[61] *Op. cit.,* v. 8, janvier 1769, p. 225.
[62] *Ibid.,* 15 avril 1769, p. 329.
[64] *Op. cit.,* v. 10, 1er juillet 1772, p. 6.
[63] *Ibid.,* octobre 1774, p. 503.
[65] Mai 1769, p. 144.

doni. A critic like Grimm was the first to congratulate an author. He professes great admiration for Sedaine's *la Gageure imprévue* (1768).

> Cette petite pièce est un chef-d'oeuvre de finesse et de plaisanterie. . . . Personne n'entend, comme M. Sedaine, l'art de manier un sujet. Tout chez lui est prévu, préparé, combiné, profondément raisonné. . . . Il a un art particulier de faire connaître ses personnages, sans avoir recours à ses fades et plates tirades qu'on place ordinairement au commencement d'une pièce, contre toute vraisemblance, pour l'instruction du spectateur.

In fact, the only reproach which Grimm makes is that the play would have gained if the author had found "un moyen de nouer plus fortement l'intrigue de la petite fille à l'intrigue principale."[66] In 1773 Sedaine wrote a guardian-ward comedy, *le Magnifique*. The comedy was based on a story of La Fontaine which had also furnished La Motte with a comedy bearing the same title. Although there are some inevitable resemblances between the two plays, there is a main difference which Sedaine himself points out: "Son Aldobrandin (le tuteur) est dupé par tout ce qui l'entoure, le mien au contraire a trompé tout le monde par une fausse probité."[67]

Sedaine was one of the eighteenth century's few real dramatists and, like every real dramatist, was keenly sensitive to the articulate and inarticulate demands of his public. Had his relations with the Comédie-Française been less strained, he might very well have won the case for the *comédie d'intrigue* and at the same time come a little closer to the aspirations of critics like Grimm.

The nearer one approaches Beaumarchais the greater becomes the preoccupation with plot. In 1770 a new comedy of Cailhava, *le Nouveau marié,* elicits the comment of Grimm who notes Cailhava's desire to revive the farce and admits that he would have succeeded long ago if his talent equaled his zeal.[68] Three years later there was a very successful revival of Cailhava's *Tuteur dupé.* Grimm believes that its great merit is its gayety.

[66] *Op. cit.,* v. 8, 1er juin 1768, pp. 89–91, *passim.*
[67] *Le Magnifique,* 1773, Avertissement.
[68] *Op. cit.,* v. 9, 1er octobre 1770, p. 130.

On désirerait sans doute que l'intrigue du *Tuteur dupé* fût plus vraisemblable . . . on voudrait enfin que toutes les scènes fussent travaillées
avec moins de négligence : mais on ne saurait refuser à l'auteur des saillies d'une verve vraiment comique, l'art d'inventer des situations plaisantes, et celui de nouer et de dénouer vivement une intrigue.[69]

Cailhava would probably have silenced his critics if he had had
some dramatic genius. The public was interested in the *comédie
d'intrigue,* social conditions favored its development rather than
that of any other comic *genre,* the critic was clamoring for a substantial plot in any kind of comedy and would be lenient enough in
his judgment of a play where plot was sought for its own sake,
provided, of course, the result were skillfully obtained. Cailhava's
own specific attempts to respond to this demand were supported by
those of Bret, Rochon de Chabannes, Barthe and Sedaine, each of
whom considered plot of sufficient importance to justify his interest in the pure *comédie d'intrigue.* The great need was for a writer
who could succeed in fixing the form of the new comedy as none
of these writers had succeeded. The dramatist capable of rising to
this supreme effort would hold in his grasp potential control over
the comedy of the future.

Beaumarchais did not at once perceive the situation and his lack
of immediate perception is extremely significant. Because Beaumarchais is the greatest dramatic genius which the eighteenth century can boast, we tend to think of him as independent of the me-
diocrities of his time; he rises so high above them that it seems
presumptuous to pin him down to a concrete background. Yet few
dramatists owe more to the epoch which they epitomize.

It is obviously not our purpose to minimize the dramatic genius
of Beaumarchais. Such an undertaking would be as absurd as it
would be fruitless. We have sought rather to ascertain the conditions which evoked his magnificent response and to increase
thereby our understanding of the dramatic evolution which he con-
summated.

Beaumarchais' dramatic interests follow the dramatic interests of
the second half of the century. If we are to believe Beaumarchais,

[69] *Op. cit.,* v. 10, avril 1773, p. 222.

he amused himself with scattered notes on "le drame sérieux" some eight years before the composition of his *Essai sur le genre dramatique sérieux,* that is, before 1759. His interest in the *genre* at that time inspired him to put his theories into practice; the difficulty of this self-imposed task prevented its accomplishment until he had before him the model of Diderot's *Père de famille.*[70] If Beaumarchais had had the project in mind before the publication of *le Père de famille,* it required an unusually long time after Diderot's works were in circulation to get it into print. Whether or not this confession of Beaumarchais' be true, the fact remains that Diderot's publication preceded his.

After a second unsuccessful experience with *le drame,* Beaumarchais turned his attention to the *comédie d'intrigue.* We have seen that the efforts of Bret, Rochon de Chabannes, Barthe, Sedaine, and especially Cailhava to restore the *genre* all precede in chronology the first representation of *le Barbier de Séville.* Cailhava's *Tuteur dupé* had enjoyed a successful revival in 1773. It is impossible to prove conclusively that this play influenced Beaumarchais' choice of subject. Literary influences are at best intangible, and unless one has the author's word for it, it is difficult to assert with positive assurance his indebtedness to another. *Le Barbier de Séville* in itself probably owes nothing to *le Tuteur dupé,* yet it would be rash to conclude that the movement of which the latter play was a manifestation was without influence in directing Beaumarchais' thoughts to the same *genre.*

Finally, animated by a new conception, Beaumarchais reverts to his original interest in the *drame.* He reconciles his first and second conceptions of the theater and asserts that incorporation in the *drame* of the main elements of the *comédie d'intrigue* will increase the excellence of the former. But Diderot, with less precision, to be sure, had already intimated this ideal and it underlies a great deal of Grimm's criticism. One cannot otherwise explain the latter's criticism, on the one hand, of a play which lacks plot and his refusal, on the other, to admit the supremacy of one where plot is sought for its own sake.

We have already seen how Beaumarchais accepts his contempo-

---

[70] *Essai sur le genre dramatique sérieux,* 1767, pp. i–iii.

raries' notion that slight opportunity remains for the writer of comedy to portray character. His exposition in the preface to *le Mariage de Figaro* of the difficulties experienced by the dramatist desirous of satirizing contemporary manners reflects the attitude of Linguet. Every class of society resents criticism on the stage. "On ne jouerait point *les Fâcheux, les Marquis, les Emprunteurs de Molière,* sans révolter à la fois la haute, la moyenne, la moderne et l'antique Noblesse."[71] Vices and abuses are eternal and disguise themselves in a thousand ways. The noble task of the dramatist is to tear away this mask and expose to public ridicule the evils it disguises.[72] Beaumarchais, like Diderot, is constantly preoccupied with the moral aim of the theater. Nevertheless this preoccupation does not seriously affect the value which he assigned to plot and its construction.

While we are primarily concerned with comedy, we cannot neglect Beaumarchais' earliest theories concerning the *drame*. Each of his prefaces marks a distinct advance over the one which precedes it and so forms an integral part of his whole theory. To understand fully the last, one must have studied the first.

We have Beaumarchais' own statements for the fact that his first theories owe much to the treatises of Diderot.[73] This is true and unfortunately so because Diderot's influence was as indelible as it was complete. One of Beaumarchais' reasons for subscribing to the *drame* as conceived by Diderot is that it embraces every station in life and provides the dramatist with the opportunity for treating anew characters exhausted by pure comedy. The beauty of the *drame,* however, is not to be found in its characters; on the contrary, "il doit tirer toute sa beauté du fond, de la texture, de l'intérêt et de la marche du sujet."[74] In this case, the subject of Beaumarchais' play is the despair to which an innocent young girl can be driven by the folly and wickedness of another person. Once the subject has been chosen, Beaumarchais admits, "J'ai chargé ce tableau d'incidens qui pouvoient encore en augmenter l'intérêt . . ."[75]

---

[71] *Préface du Mariage de Figaro,* III, 6. (d'Heylli, de Marescot edition. Unless otherwise stated, references to Beaumarchais have been taken from this edition.) For Linguet, cf. p. 88 of this chapter.
[72] *Ibid.,* p. 9.
[73] *Essai sur le genre dramatique sérieux,* 1767, pp. iii, xxvi, xxxiv, xli.
[74] *Ibid.,* p. xxx.　　　　　　[75] *Ibid.,* p. xxxiv.

He prides himself on having condensed the plot to include the least possible number of actors. The relation of the characters to this subject is determined after the manner of Diderot. He has not given to his hero, his heroine, and their accomplices characters chosen at random or characters mutually antithetical for, as Diderot has proved, this device is trivial and at best suited only to comedy. No, Beaumarchais has chosen his characters so that they may contribute "de la manière la plus naturelle à renforcer l'intérêt principal qui porte sur Eugénie : et combinant ensuite le jeu de tous ces caractères avec le fond de mon roman, j'ai trouvé, pour résultat, le fil de la conduite que chacun y devait tenir . . ."[76] This, of course, is another way of saying with Diderot, "c'est aux situations à décider des caractères."[77] It seems incredible that Beaumarchais' dramatic instinct did not preserve him from falling into the error of Diderot. This fundamental misconception of the art of the drama illustrates the extent to which Beaumarchais shared eighteenth century tradition and explains in great measure his lack of success with the *drame* and his success, on the other hand, with the *comédie d'intrigue*. His subordination of character to the situation he wishes to present in his *drame* determined at the outset its failure. While the subordination of character to plot may not be an indispensable requisite for the success of the *comédie d'intrigue*, it in no way restricts that success.

Encouraged perhaps by his contemporaries' relative successes with the *comédie d'intrigue*, Beaumarchais temporarily abandons his plans for the *drame* to concern himself with a play in which

---

[76] *Ibid.*, p. xxxiv.

[77] It is Lintilhac's opinion that Beaumarchais' stand was mid-way between the extreme of Diderot and the formal contradiction of Diderot's principle by Mercier who says, ". . . l'action jaillit du jeu des caractères." With Beaumarchais, the situations and the characters "réagiront les uns sur les autres"; in support of his conclusion Lintilhac cites this passage from the preface to *Eugénie* to the effect that "tout homme est lui-même par son caractère et qu'il est ce qu'il plaît au sort par son état sur lequel ce caractère influe beaucoup. . . ." So far as I can see, however, the first statement has no counterpart in the prefaces of Beaumarchais and the context of the passage cited in its support invalidates the statement for me. Beaumarchais used these words not in discussing the relation of his characters to the situation in the play but in establishing the fact that, since a man in life is what he is by his character and since his station in life is determined by chance, it is that character rather than his station in life which should arouse the dramatist's interest; "d'où il suit (and these are the words which immediately follow those cited by Lintilhac) que le Drame sérieux, qui me présente des

plot is sought for its own sake. He had no other motive than to write an amusing comedy, a kind of *imbroille*,[78] and to bring back to the theater with his *Barbier de Séville* its time-honored, frank gayety.[79]

Beaumarchais' second comedy, *le Mariage de Figaro,* represents not a pure *comédie d'intrigue* but the union of all traditional comic *genres*. Nevertheless his evident desire to give vent to political and social satire does not absorb his interest in plot as such nor does it dispel his knowledge of its value. His primary objection to the pedantic abuse of the words, *bon ton, bonne compagnie, décence et bonnes moeurs* by hypersensitive critics is that such abuse fetters genius, intimidates all authors, and strikes "un coup mortel à la vigueur de l'intrigue, sans laquelle il n'y a pourtant que du bel esprit à la glace et des comédies de quatre jours."[80] Beaumarchais was carried away by his overambitiousness, and his play suffered somewhat in consequence. The plot, however, is substantial, perhaps too substantial, and forms an integral part of the whole.

Beaumarchais' last dramatic production, *la Mère coupable,* is entitled "drame moral." If we are to believe its author, his two comedies merely served as preparation for this last composition. In his discussion of the play, he gives us his final word on the value of plot. Simply stated, his play is composed of "une intrigue de comédie, fondue dans le pathétique d'un drame." In the opinion of some critics, the latter *genre* does not permit the union of these two elements. Plot, they hold, is characteristic of gay subjects, the particular possession of comedy; the pathetic should be adapted to the simple action of the *drame*. These principles fade away in the process of application, as any author knows who has tried both *genres*. It is Beaumarchais' conclusion that "le mélange heureux de ces deux moyens dramatiques employés avec art peut produire un très-grand effet." In his own play, *"la comédie d'intrigue,* soutenant la curiosité, marche tout au travers *du drame,* dont elle ren-

---

hommes vivement affectés par un événement, est susceptible d'autant de nerf, de force, ou d'élévation que la Tragédie héroïque, qui me montre aussi des hommes vivement affectés, dans des conditions seulement plus relevées." (*Essai sur le genre dramatique sérieux,* 1767, p. xxiv), (Lintilhac, *Beaumarchais et ses oeuvres,* 1887, pp. 311–312.)

[78] *Lettre modérée sur la chute et la critique du Barbier de Séville,* II, 11.
[79] *Préface du Mariage de Figaro,* III, 10–11.
[80] *Ibid.,* p. 6.

force l'action, sans en diviser l'intérêt, qui se porte tout entier sur
la mère."[81]

The moral aim which is to dominate his play sounds strangely
like that of the *comédie à thèse* perfected in the nineteenth century: ". . . *la Mère coupable* est un tableau des peines intérieures
qui divisent bien des familles. . . . Le sentiment de la paternité,
la bonté du coeur, l'indulgence, en sont les remèdes. Voilà ce que
j'ai voulu peindre et graver dans tous les esprits."[82] Whether or
not he accomplishes his intentions, Beaumarchais claims that the
aim he has proposed is none the less true; his example will inspire
others who may be more successful.

> Qu'un homme de fer l'entreprenne, y mêlant, d'un crayon hardi, *l'in-
> trigue* avec le *pathétique*. Qu'il broie et fonde savamment les vives cou-
> leurs de chacun; qu'il nous peigne à grands traits l'homme vivant en
> société, son état, ses passions, ses vices, ses vertus, ses fautes et ses mal-
> heurs . . . Touchés, intéressés, instruits, nous ne dirons plus que le
> drame est un genre décoloré, né de l'impuissance de produire une tragé-
> die ou une comédie. L'art aura pris un noble essor; il aura fait encore un
> pas.[83]

The analogies between this theory of Beaumarchais and those of
Augier and Dumas *fils* are striking enough to encourage the conclusion that the nineteenth century dramatists were indebted to the
former for their conception of the theater. Nevertheless, such a
conclusion would probably be unwarranted. Similarities in the
theories of Beaumarchais and those of Dumas *fils* and Augier
probably result from a like reaction to a given situation rather than
from direct influence of the one on the others. Once Beaumarchais
became convinced of the importance of a well-constructed plot,
once he had perfected the vehicle for his ideas, it was natural for
him to desire the use of that vehicle to embody his ideas. Likewise,
once Scribe had demonstrated the value resulting from a flawlessly
constructed plot, once he had perfected an instrument for dramatic
propaganda, it was natural enough for dramatists of a different
type to seize upon that instrument for social and moral purposes.

Beaumarchais and one or two discerning critics like Grimm and

---

[81] *Un Mot sur la Mère coupable,* IV, 199, 200. The first manuscript of this
play bears the title "Drame intrigué" (cf. Lintilhac, *op. cit.,* p. 289).
[82] *Ibid.,* p. 199.   [83] *Ibid.,* p. 201.

Fréron had vision enough to see that plot for its own sake is not the highest aim of dramatic art. As we shall see more definitely later, the eighteenth century on the whole lacked this vision. Its immediate problem was the perfecting of the dramatic vehicle in practice as well as in theory and the shifting of dramatic emphasis to the side of plot-construction. Had Beaumarchais been able to rise in practice above the eighteenth century's general conception of the theater to the ideal which he himself expressed in his last preface, he might have succeeded in diverting the eighteenth century's attention from the purely mechanical side of a play to something deeper.

His own prefaces reflect the eighteenth century's interest in the mechanical construction of a play and are excellent examples of the extent to which playwriting was becoming a *métier*. Throughout the greater part of his career, Beaumarchais' interest in a play is largely of a technical nature. Even in the *Essai sur le genre dramatique sérieux,* where the aim is presumably to justify presentation on the stage of a new subject-matter, Beaumarchais' underscoring of technical reforms recommended by Diderot is one of the most outstanding characteristics. Nor does he forget these ideas with his temporary cessation of interest in the *drame,* for they recur in part in the prefaces to his comedies and, as everyone familiar with his plays will recognize, they recur in whole in the comedies themselves.

One of Diderot's first admonitions to the dramatist was that he should make adequate preparation for the incidents of his play. One is conscious of Beaumarchais' efforts to carry out this suggestion. He admits himself,

si mon Drame n'est pas mieux fait, c'est moins parce que j'ai marché en aveugle dans un pays perdu, que pour avoir mal exécuté ce que j'avais beaucoup combiné. . . . Ceux qui liront *Eugénie* . . . sentiront souvent que l'Auteur a plus réfléchi qu'on ne croit, lorsqu'il a préféré de dire plus en peu de mots, que mieux en beaucoup de paroles. Alors le premier Acte, qu'ils avaient peut-être trouvé long et froid, leur paraîtra si nécessaire, qu'il serait impossible de prendre le moindre intérêt aux autres si l'on n'avait pas vu celui-là.[84]

[84] *Essai sur le genre dramatique sérieux,* 1767, pp. xxxiii, lx.

To be sure, seventeenth century theorists, d'Aubignac for example, were aware of the value of preparation, but it does not carry with them the premium it had come to acquire by the end of the eighteenth century. Cailhava insists that the spectator wishes to have in his hands, "avant la fin du premier acte, les fils de tous les ressorts de la machine, sans deviner les effets qu'ils produiront."[85] This art of preparation is the whole art of the "pièce bien faite."

Beaumarchais underlines Diderot's attention to small details and his desire to counterbalance extraordinary events by apparently insignificant details. The most moving scenes of *Eugénie* are aroused by a crisis

> d'autant plus pénible pour le spectateur, qu'il l'a vue se former lentement sous ses yeux, et par des moyens communs et foibles en apparence. . . . Plus il y a de choses fortes ou extraordinaires dans un Drame, et plus on doit les racheter par des incidens communs, qui seuls forment la vérité. (C'est encore M. Diderot qui dit cela.) Que ne dit-il pas, cet homme étonnant![86]

Likewise, Beaumarchais seems to approve Diderot's idea that the characters of a play should be kept in a constant state of turmoil by the play and interplay of action. It is the successful application of this suggestion which most clearly distinguishes *le Barbier de Séville* from previous guardian-ward comedies. The guardian in the average comedy has little ingenuity. There is a single rising line of action which carries the lovers successfully to the end. Beaumarchais, too, like Fréron, Diderot, Grimm and Sedaine, must have recognized the languor which this brings about in the action of the play. He definitely points out his attempt to avoid this result in *le Barbier de Séville:* "de cela seul que le Tuteur est un peu moins sot que tous ceux qu'on trompe au Théâtre, il a résulté beaucoup de mouvement dans la Pièce, et sur-tout la nécessité d'y donner plus de ressort aux intriguants."[87] Consequently Almaviva must take infinite pains to establish himself "dans un fort défendu par la vigilance et le soupçon, (et) sur-tout à tromper un

---

[85] Cf. p. 96 in this chapter.
[86] *Essai sur le genre dramatique sérieux,* 1767, pp. xl–xli.
[87] *Lettre modérée sur la chute et la critique du Barbier de Séville,* II, 11. For Diderot's idea see pp. 70–71, n. 73, of this dissertation.

homme qui, sans cesse éventant la manoeuvre, oblige l'ennemi de se retourner assez lestement pour n'être pas désarçonné d'emblée."[88] The fact that they play into each other's hands keeps the characters in a constant state of turmoil; "le Tuteur a fermé sa porte en donnant son passe-partout à Bazile, pour que lui seul et le Notaire puissent entrer et conclure son mariage";[89] and he finds himself forced to exclaim at the end, "Et moi qui leur ai enlevé l'échelle pour que le mariage fût plus sûr!"[90] Nor can one overlook "l'embarras où l'Auteur s'est jeté volontairement au dernier Acte, en faisant avouer par la Pupille à son Tuteur que le Comte avait dérobé la clef de la jalousie; et comment l'Auteur s'en démêle en deux mots et sort, en se jouant de la nouvelle inquiétude qu'il a imprimée au Spectateur."[91]

Beaumarchais tries to apply the same principle in *le Mariage de Figaro,* although the result is not quite so neat. He chooses in order to keep Almaviva alert

> l'homme le plus dégourdi de sa nation, *le véritable Figaro,* qui, . . . se moque des projets de son maître et s'indigne très-plaisamment qu'il ose joûter de ruse avec lui, maître passé dans ce genre d'escrime.
>
> Ainsi d'une lutte assez vive entre l'abus et la puissance, l'oubli des principes, la prodigalité, l'occasion, tout ce que la séduction a de plus entraînant; et le feu, l'esprit, les ressources que l'infériorité piquée au jeu peut opposer à cette attaque, il naît dans ma Pièce un jeu plaisant d'intrigue, où *l'époux suborneur* . . . toujours arrêté dans ses vues, est obligé, trois fois dans cette journée de tomber aux pieds de sa femme . . .[92]

Diderot advocated the replacing of surprise technique by one of suspense, and Beaumarchais continually alludes to the same principle. One of the main reasons for the interest which Beaumarchais' *drame* arouses is that he has informed the spectator of the respective situations and intentions of all the characters. Heretofore authors have taken as many pains to secure momentary surprises as Beaumarchais has to secure suspense. He acknowledges, ". . . célèbre Diderot, c'est vous qui le premier avez fait une regle

---

[88] *Ibid.,* p. 15.   [89] *Ibid.,* p. 15.
[90] *Le Barbier de Séville,* IV, 8.
[91] *Lettre modérée sur la chute et la critique du Barbier de Séville,* II, 16.
[92] *Préface du Mariage de Figaro,* III, 14.

dramatique de ce moyen sûr et rapide de remuer l'ame des spectateurs. J'avais osé le prévoir dans mon plan; mais c'est la lecture de
votre immortel Ouvrage qui m'a rassuré sur son effet."[93] And he
adduces the same reasons as Diderot in support of this principle. In
the eyes of the spectator, the two young people in *la Mère coupable*
do not run the risk of meeting any real danger. It is apparent that
they will be married, provided the villain is ejected, for they are
not at all related to each other, "ce que savent fort bien, dans le
secret du coeur, le comte, la comtesse, le scélérat, Suzanne et Figaro, tous instruits des événemens, sans compter le public qui as-
siste à la pièce, et à qui nous n'avons rien caché."[94]

On the other hand, a passage from a letter on *la Mère coupable*
seems to indicate that Beaumarchais was less adamant than Diderot[95] in regard to the technique of suspense versus that of surprise:
"Ce qui met, selon moi, de l'intérêt jusqu'au dernier mot, dans une
pièce, est *l'accumulement successif de tous les genres d'inquiétudes
que l'auteur sait verser dans l'âme du spectateur, pour l'en sortir
après d'une manière inattendue! Cette anxiété perpétuelle est un
moyen de s'emparer de lui.*"[96] He wishes to relieve the spectator's
anxiety in an unexpected manner. Nevertheless this does not necessarily mean that the author is going to withhold from the spectator
all the strings of his plot. Even though the spectator holds all the
strings, he may still be unable to see the way in which they are to
be unraveled. This happened in the case of *le Barbier de Séville*
and Beaumarchais rails against the critic who has dared to call
Bartholo stupid for not having foreseen "une intrigue dont on lui
cachait tout, lorsque lui, critique, *à qui l'on ne cachait rien, ne l'a
pas devinée plus que le Tuteur.*"[97]

Finally, Diderot had urged the concentration of action in a play
by the elimination of extraneous material. Beaumarchais had already adopted this principle in his original four-act draft of *le
Barbier de Séville*.[98] The public present at the initial performance
of the five-act version forced him to delete the extraneous passages
which his desire for satirical vengeance had meanwhile inspired

[93] *Essai sur le genre dramatique sérieux*, 1767, pp. xxxviii–xxxix.
[94] *Un Mot sur la Mère coupable*, IV, 200.
[95] Cf. Lintilhac, *op. cit.*, p. 316. [96] *Ibid.*, Appendice, No. 40, p. 426.
[97] *Lettre modérée sur la chute et la critique du Barbier de Séville*, II, 16.
[98] Cf. Introduction, p. 2.

him to insert. The lively manner in which he describes this revision rivals the play itself in merriment.[99]

Thus we see that by (1) his direct allusions to the value of preparation, (2) his desire to counterbalance extraordinary events with apparently insignificant details, (3) his belief that the characters of a play should be kept in a constant state of turmoil by the play and interplay of action, (4) his faith in the advantages to be derived from the technique of suspense rather than surprise, and (5) his ultimate decision to concentrate the action of *le Barbier de Séville* by eliminating unnecessary details, Beaumarchais underscores in his prefaces and in his practice some of the technical reforms advocated by Diderot.

It seems exaggerated to attribute the excellent construction of *le Barbier de Séville* to a direct influence of Diderot. Beaumarchais had dramatic talent; Diderot did not. Yet the former's express admission, as the passages quoted above have illustrated, of the importance of Diderot's technical reforms would seem to indicate a conscious adoption of the latter's suggestions. On the other hand, resultant similarities in theory and practice may be due to pure chance. Beaumarchais' own technical insight might very well have led him independently to the conclusions expressed in his prefaces. But if this study has shown anything, it has shown that Beaumarchais' successful technical innovations were not the result of unconscious dramatic genius. Technical devices are deliberately discussed in his prefaces. This fact indicates, too, the extent to which Beaumarchais was interested in the mechanical construction of a play, and it is noteworthy that he failed almost completely when he attempted any dramatic *genre* requiring something more than technical skill. He says himself: "La théorie de l'art peut être le fruit de l'étude et des réflexions; mais l'exécution appartient au génie, qui ne s'apprend point."[100] The element which has made a few dramas works of art is known only to genius and cannot be transmitted or defined in tangible terms. The same cannot be said for the *métier* of the drama. French dramatists did not succeed in surpassing, or even equaling, the art in Molière's *comédies de carac-*

---

[99] *Lettre modérée sur la chute et la critique du Barbier de Séville*, II. 19–20.
[100] *Essai sur le genre dramatique sérieux*, 1767, p. xxxii.

tère, but they did learn how to improve upon his *métier,* the technical construction of his plays, to such an extent that the mechanics of playwriting became for a time the sole aim of the theater. In view of these facts, it does not seem too hazardous to conclude that Diderot probably whetted in Beaumarchais a consciousness of his own technical abilities which he might not otherwise have felt.

Although one occasionally finds a dissenting voice,[101] the majority of contemporary critics show an intelligent appreciation of *le Barbier de Séville.* The most penetrating criticism is that of Grimm for whom the chief merit of the play lies in "la finesse des ressorts qui lient l'intrigue . . . Cette comédie, sans être du meilleur genre, sans avoir non plus la verve et la folie des farces de Molière, n'est pas moins l'ouvrage d'un homme de beaucoup d'esprit . . . Toute l'intrigue est liée avec adresse, et le dénoûment en est ingénieux."[102] At the end of the year his opinion is the same: "Nous ne craindrons point de dire que cette pièce peut être mise à côté des meilleures farces de Molière, que si le fond en est moins philosophique, l'intrigue en est plus adroite, et que les plus grands maîtres de l'art n'auraient point désavoué la scène de Bazile."[103]

Grimm, and there were others like him, still maintained that whatever perfection the *genre* might attain, it was still not of the best. In general, however, critics and authors, who may not have appreciated the full import of *le Barbier de Séville,* were unable to resist the movement of which it was the chief and best manifestation. Cailhava very likely expresses the average opinion when he says in his *De l'Art de la comédie,* a fairly popular work,[104]

Rien de plus plaisant que le souverain mépris qu'on affecte pour les *pieces d'intrigue* . . . Il est sans doute plus beau, plus grand de faire une piece à *caractere;* mais elle est défectueuse si *l'intrigue* n'en lie les différents portraits . . . Je vous prédis donc que vous ne réussirez jamais à faire une bonne piece à *caractere,* si vous ne commencez par vous exercer dans les sentiers compliqués d'une *intrigue* adroite et vigoureuse.[105]

Even more interesting are the opinions expressed in the *Diction-*

[101] Cf. for example, *le Nouveau Spectateur,* 1775, troisième cahier, p. 34 f.
[102] *Op. cit.,* v. 11, mars 1775, pp. 52-53.
[103] *Ibid.,* décembre 1775, p. 168.   [104] Gaiffe, *op. cit.,* p. 132, n. 2.
[105] 1772, v. 2, p. 123.

naire dramatique of La Porte and Chamfort. La Porte reiterates what had already been said in 1749[106] in the *Lettres sur quelques écrits de ce tems:* "Les Piéces de caractère sont plus goûtées aujourd'hui, que les Piéces d'intrigue; parce que ces derniers ne sont que l'ombre de la vérité, et que les autres en sont une fidele image."[107] In 1749, the critic believed that the art of constructing a plot "appartient également aux pièces de caracteres; parce que l'intrigue est la base du genre dramatique. Sans intrigue, point de Comédie." In 1776, he is more convinced of the correctness of his opinion and has become more emphatic because he adds to what was true in 1749 what is now true in 1776: "Plusieurs Auteurs ont prétendu qu'une Comédie de caractère n'étoit pas susceptible d'intrigue, ou du moins qu'elle n'en admettoit qu'une très légère. Il paroît qu'une Comédie dénuée d'intrigue sera toujours défectueuse . . . ."[108] Everything should be in action, even the exposition.[109] He goes so far as to concede later, "L'intrigue est la partie la plus essentielle pour entretenir l'attentior. et soutenir l'intérêt de curiosité."[110] The author betrays his time, too, when he observes, "s'il faut éviter une Action chargée d'intrigues et d'évenemens, il faut prendre garde aussi que l'extrême simplicité ne rende le Sujet nud et stérile."[111]

The comedies of Beaumarchais were all that was needed to increase the force of the movement. This fact did not escape La Harpe who observes in connection with *le Mariage de Figaro* that "à force d'aimer le changement et la nouveauté, nous revenons précisément au point d'où nous étions partis. Tout le monde sait qu'avant Molière, tous nos auteurs comiques empruntaient leurs intrigues du théâtre espagnol, chaos de situations forcées, où l'on comptait pour rien le bon sens, les moeurs et la vraisemblance." Although he concludes that the play is "un monstre dramatique, . . . (elle) n'en est pas moins susceptible d'un succès dont le dangereux exemple irait à nous ramener à l'enfance de l'art."[112]

[106] Cf. Ch. II, p. 24. La Porte collaborated with Fréron for some of the volumes of this journal. If he himself did not write this passage, he was very likely familiar with it.

[107] *Dictionnaire dramatique,* 1776, v. 1, p. 215.

[108] *Ibid.,* p. 216.   [109] *Ibid.,* p. 462.

[110] *Ibid.,* v. 2, p. 85.   [111] *Ibid.,* v. 1. p. 20.

[112] *Correspondance littéraire,* 1801, v. 4, Lettre CLXXXIX (n.d.) pp. 122–123, *passim.*

The situation had become general enough two or three years later to elicit the comment of Marmontel who, by his own classical reaction, gives us an accurate idea of the extent to which the movement had been carried and the value which plot had assumed in the eyes of his contemporaries.

> Le premier procédé de l'art de la Comédie, a été d'ajuster ensemble des événemens propres à exciter le rire. . . . Mais *ce moyen de l'art n'en étoit pas la fin;* et c'est à quoi l'art s'est mépris lui-même dans son enfance, lorsqu'il n'avoit encore l'idée ni de sa puissance ni de sa dignité: *c'est à quoi, dans sa décadence, il se méprend encore,* lorsque les grands talens qui l'avoient porté à son comble, n'existent plus pour l'y soutenir, et que les grands principes du goût . . . ont disparu avec les grands talens.

If a series of amusing surprises and misunderstandings alone constituted good comedy, *l'Etourdi* and *le Cocu imaginaire* would be preferable to *le Misanthrope, le Légataire* would be at least the equal of *le Tartuffe.* This is not the case. Nothing is livelier on the stage than Spanish and Italian comedy, yet Molière ceased imitating Spanish and Italian models as soon as he felt his own powers. "Il reconnut que *l'action* comique tiroit sa force et sa beauté des moeurs; et que, pour faire rire les honnêtes gens, c'étoit à l'esprit qu'il devoit s'adresser, moins par les yeux que par l'oreille."

In spite of his classical tendencies, it is noteworthy that Marmontel concedes, "Je ne dis pas que la même *action* ne puisse en même temps parler aux yeux et à l'esprit: si elle réunit ces deux moyens, l'impression n'en est que plus vive; et c'est peut-être un avantage qu'on a trop souvent négligé." If one must choose, however, between a play which appeals to the eye and one which appeals to the mind, there is neither excuse nor reason for hesitation. The first will have its success, but it will be "le succès de la pantomime, après laquelle il ne reste rien. Ainsi, celui qui, après avoir rempli un canevas de pantomime, nous dira que sa pièce est faite pour être jouée et non pour être lue, se placera lui-même dans le nombre de compositeurs de ballets."[113]

[113] *Oeuvres complettes,* 1787, v. 5, *Elémens de littérature,* tome premier, Article—Action, pp. 72–80, *passim.* (Italics mine.)

It is difficult to believe that these passages are contemporaneous with Beaumarchais and that over two decades are to elapse before Scribe appears on the scene. In one sense, the fears of La Harpe and Marmontel are well founded; they perceived with accuracy the course which comedy had adopted and which it gave every promise of following. In another sense, their criticism is the result of unnecessarily exaggerated misapprenensions. They either could not or would not see the difference distinguishing later eighteenth century comedy from that of the early seventeenth century. More than ever before critics and authors are concerned with the exposition of comedy, the elimination of unnecessary details, the preparation of incidents, the artistic arrangement of scenes and acts and a logical *dénouement*.

For Cailhava the arrangement of the exposition influences the whole play. Authors can no longer proceed as Plautus did and inform the spectator by means of a prologue about everything which is to happen; that method, as Molière very well knew, destroys the interest of the audience. The exposition should be short, rapid, and clear; the audience wishes to know promptly the events which have preceded the action and the place where this action will occur and they do not wish to have this information unnaturally given to some useless character.[114] Above all, the exposition should not be cluttered with portraits foreign to the subject or with details which serve no purpose.[115]

The avoidance of unnecessary details in the exposition should extend to the rest of the play. Bret's *l'Orpheline ou le Faux généreux* was originally a five-act play. The author has since reduced it to three acts and hopes thereby that "la fable de l'ouvrage plus serrée, et plus rapprochée, produira plus d'effet."[116] Marin admits that he will be reproached for "des répétitions, des longueurs . . ."[117] *L'Encyclopédie* affirms that an author no longer has any authorization for inserting episodes in his play, especially when

---

[114] *Théâtre*, 1781, v. 2, p. 469.
[115] *De l'Art de la comédie*, 1772, v. 1, pp. 157–158.
[116] *Oeuvres de théâtre*, 1765, *l'Orpheline ou le Faux généreux*, Avertissement, p. 318.
[117] *Pièces de théâtre*, 1765, *Julie ou le Triomphe de l'amitié*, Observations sur cette pièce, p. 69.

they concern only secondary characters.[118] The *Mercure de France* praises Sedaine's *le Philosophe sans le savoir* because there is not a word which does not bear some necessary relation to the main interest of the play.[119] This journal believes, also, that in Barthe's *les Fausses infidélités* the action "n'est jamais retardée par des accessoires étrangers; point de scène épisodique, point d'ornemens superflus . . ."[120]

If the dramatist has carefully prepared for and motivated the incidents of his comedy, he will not be criticised for useless scenes and pointless repetitions. Grimm admires Sedaine because he prepares for his dramatic effects with so much skill. "Le grand art de M. Sedaine consiste à méditer longtemps son sujet, à le couver, pour ainsi dire, et le féconder de toutes les manières possibles . . . Voyez comme tout tient au sujet, en sort et y ramène; voyez avec quel art et quel naturel les plus petits détails sont fondés . . ."[121] Cailhava's belief in the value of preparation surpasses that of Diderot and equals that of Scribe:

> On n'est jamais plus convaincu de l'art et de la profondeur d'un Comique, que lorsqu'on le voit aller avec adresse au devant des critiques que le spectateur pourroit lui faire, et le préparer d'avance à trouver bon tout ce qu'il va voir et entendre, tandis qu'il l'auroit trouvé mal sans la précaution de l'Auteur.[122]

Cailhava's words are reiterated in *le Dictionnaire dramatique* where preparation and suspense are the two great secrets of dramatic art.[123]

If the dramatist has carefully prepared the incidents of his play, they will derive one from the other; this interdependence of action will foster a compactness and unity which the play might not otherwise have had. In order to obtain the maximum effect, the dramatist should strive for the artistic arrangement of his plot. Critics frown on plays which do not thus hold together, theorists emphasize the necessity for this artistry in arrangement and dramatists

[118] V. 8, partie II, n.d. (1765), p. 574.
[119] Janvier 1766, v. 1, p. 210.   [120] Mars 1768, p. 196.
[121] *Op. cit.*, v. 6, 15 décembre 1765, pp. 439, 444.
[122] *De l'Art de la comédie*, 1772, v. 1, p. 308.
[123] 1776, v. 1, p. 138.

point to their plays with pride whenever they have succeeded in adroitly interweaving the events of their plays.[124]

Not only must each incident be the outcome of the one preceding it; the final incident, the *dénouement,* must be the logical outcome of the whole. Critics of 1760 condemned the ending of *les Philosophes* on the grounds that the author had not sufficiently justified the brusque change from implicit confidence in "les philosophes" to utter distrust. Lamarche-Courmont, Palissot's apologist, maintains that the ending was prepared for at the beginning of the third act. The arrival of Crispin is the audience's signal for they know that he bears the intercepted letter which is to bring about the ending. Lamarche-Courmont concludes: "Ce dénouement ne tombe donc pas des nues, et n'est donc point aussi puérile . . . que celui des Femmes sçavantes . . ."[125] In 1764 the *Mercure de France* observes with regard to Bret's *l'Epreuve indiscrette:* "Le retour imprévu du père a des éxemples dans les anciens, mais devient toujours forcé dans nos moeurs."[126] The following year Marmontel notes in *l'Encyclopédie* that Molière agreed on this point with the ancients. After having amused the audience for two hours by exposing to ridicule certain vices and follies, he thought that "la façon plus ou moins adroite et naturelle de terminer l'action comique, n'en devoit pas décider le succès, et qu'un père, un oncle tombé des nues à la fin de la comédie . . . suffiroit pour la dénouer." And Marmontel concludes that, while the dramatist should attempt to do better than Molière in this particular respect, he should not attribute to the "tour d'adresse d'un *dénouement* comique, un mérite comparable à celui de l'intrigue ou du Tartuffe, ou de l'Avare . . ."[127] Marmontel perceives that his contemporaries are prepared to do just this thing; subsequent theory and practice prove that his warning had no effect on the shifting change in values. Nougaret is witness to the fact that by 1769 contemporary opinion is distinctly un-

---

[124] Cf. for example, (a) *Mercure de France,* septembre 1761, p. 202.
    (b) Bachaumont, *op. cit.,* v. 16, Additions (1763), p. 183, v. 3, 26 février 1768, p. 342.
    (c) Cailhava, *op. cit.,* v. 1, pp. 168–169.
    (d) Sedaine, *Oeuvres dramatiques,* 1776, v. 1, *le Jardinier et son seigneur,* Avertissement, p. 6.
[125] *Réponse aux différens écrits publiés contre la comédie des Philosophes,* 1760, p. 73.
[126] Mars 1764, pp. 219–220.   [127] V. 10, partie II, p. 679.

favorable to an illogical *dénouement* for he maintains, "L'arrivée imprévue d'un nouvel Acteur, comme dans Molière, les miracles, les maladies, et la mort subite de quelqu'un, sont absolument à rejetter. Les reconnaissances, hormis qu'elles soient ménagées dès le commencement, font toujours un mauvais effet."[128] Cailhava and the authors of *le Dictionnaire dramatique* devote many pages to the same subject and arrive at similar conclusions.[129]

In the face of this increasing attention to *forme*, it was inevitable that the *fond* which constitutes drama's real claim to art should become of subsidiary importance. The careful, precisely calculated combinations of a scientifically constructed play pass to the level of first importance. This excessive attention to the mechanics of play-construction, first noted in the treatises of Diderot, increased until it assumed alarming proportions about the year 1775.

A very complete definition of the new attitude toward dramatic art is provided by the *Dictionnaire dramatique*. Its authors note that in addition to the principal rules of dramatic art associated with plot, interest, unity, etc., there exists

> un Art plus caché et plus délicat, qui regle en quelque façon tous les pas qu'on doit faire, et qui n'abandonne rien aux caprices du génie même. Il consiste à ranger tellement ce qu'on a à dire, que, du commencement à la fin, les choses se servent de préparation les unes aux autres, et que cependant elles ne paroissent jamais dites pour rien préparer. C'est une attention de tous les instans, à mettre si bien toutes les circonstances à leur place, qu'elles soient nécessaires où on les met, et que d'ailleurs elles s'éclaircissent et s'embellissent toutes réciproquement; à tout arranger pour les effets qu'on a en vue, sans laisser appercevoir de dessein; de maniere enfin que le Spectateur voye toujours une action, et ne sente jamais un Ouvrage.[130]

It is doubtful whether our authors would admit that they had reduced the art of the drama to the mechanics of plot-construction; one hesitates to believe that they fully realized what they were doing. They naïvely betray themselves, however, when they discuss the *plan* which should form the basis for every play. The steps

[128] *Op. cit.*, p. 201.
[129] Cailhava, *op. cit.*, v. 1, pp. 502–509; *Dictionnaire dramatique*, 1776, v. 1, pp. 356–364.
[130] V. 1, p. 133.

which the dramatist must take to produce a successful play are defined and explained with the sureness accompanying the exposition of scientific formulas:

> Il faut bien discerner le moment où l'action doit commencer et où elle doit finir ; bien choisir le noeud qui doit l'embarrasser, et l'incident principal qui doit la dénouer : considérer de quels personnages secondaires on aura besoin, pòur faire briller le principal . . . Cela fait, on divise son sujet par Actes, et les Actes par Scènes ; de maniere que chaque Acte, quelques grandes situations qu'il amene, en fasse attendre encore de plus grandes, et laisse toujours le Spectateur dans l'inquiétude de ce qui doit arriver, jusqu'à l'entier dénouement . . . il distribue les Scènes de chaque Acte, faisant venir, pour chacune, les Personnages qui y sont nécessaires, observant qu'aucun ne s'y montre sans raison . . . n'y dise que ce qui est convenable, et qui tend à augmenter l'intérêt de l'action. Les parties du Drame étant ainsi esquissés, ses Actes bien marqués, ses incidens bien ménagés et enchaînés les uns aux autres, ses Scènes bien liées, bien amenées, tous ses caractères bien dessinés, il ne reste plus au Poëte, que les Vers à faire.[131]

About 1775 it was suggestions like these which the dramatist was required to carry out. It is remarkable that Scribe, the greatest exponent of this conception of dramatic art, did nothing more.

The attitude, of course, is a continuation of the one already assumed by Diderot. In fact, its authors glibly repeat with Diderot, "Le plan d'un Drame peut être fait, et très-bien fait, sans que le Poëte sache rien encore du caractère qu'il attachera à ses Personnages."[132] The evidence is the more arresting here because the writers have no reforming pretensions. Although one must assume that it bears their approval, the dictionary is not so much a mirror of personal beliefs as a compendium of prevailing contemporary opinion. To me, these passages are irrefutable proof that by 1775 the attitude of Diderot has become common property, so much so, in fact, that one is not surprised to find Marmontel, an author with classical tendencies, ask in 1787 : ". . . dans un ouvrage où tout doit se lier, sè combiner comme dans une montre, pour produire un effet commun, est-il prudent de se livrer à son génie, sans avoir son *Plan* sous les yeux ?"[133]

[131] *Ibid.*, v. 2, pp. 432–433.   [132] *Ibid.*, p. 435.
[133] *Op. cit.*, v. 9, p. 288.

It is to the credit of the eighteenth century that it defined in theory and illustrated in practice the value and importance of a well-constructed plot. It is to its discredit that this secondary element should have been made the chief aim of dramatic art. Such a complete reversal of values, in a century presumably iconoclastic, but weighted down in literature by classical tradition, is not the result of chance nor the work of a single man, but the cumulative work of several generations. The most outstanding name is that of Beaumarchais because it was he who exemplified the ultimate ideal of the century. His predecessors—Beaumarchais would probably be the first to agree with them—can legitimately appropriate as their own these words of Palissot : "Tout le monde a des yeux pour voir les abus ; la gloire de les détruire est réservée à des mains plus habiles. (Nous avons) cru pouvoir essayer d'en faire naître l'idée."[134]

[134] *Les Tuteurs,* 1755, Discours préliminaire, p. xxv.

CONCLUSION

The seventeenth century bequeathed to the eighteenth century the classical conception of comedy; this meant, of course, comedy as conceived by Molière, comedy where the chief preoccupation was character-study and the portrayal of contemporary manners rather than an impeccably constructed plot. By the time of Beaumarchais the plot of comedy was no longer of incidental importance; it had become an integral and essential part of every good play. Beaumarchais, it is true, did more than any other one man to impose the form of the new comedy but the way had been opened by a century of preparation.

We have attempted to present the gradual breaking down and undermining of the old ideals and conceptions and the substitution and building up of the new. The process was effected by a continuous development from the early efforts of Lesage to infuse life into the contemporary *comédie de caractère* and the *comédie de moeurs* to the time when a perfected *comédie d'intrigue* had replaced both these *genres*.

The suggestions of Lesage were not particularly fruitful but they indicate, along with other manifestations of discontent during the first two or three decades of the eighteenth century, an approaching change in attitude.

The following years are marked by the persistent efforts of Destouches to revive the classical *comédie de caractère*. Destouches started out with the best of intentions and succeeded in renewing the classical *comédie de caractère,* for a time at any rate, by introducing into it romanesque incidents and a more complicated action. He ended by admitting that a comedy "et d'intrigue et de caractère" had the greatest chance for success. He helped transform thereby the attitude toward comedy. What had become an important element for Destouches became a still more important element for one of his immediate successors, La Chaussée. By the middle of the century the preoccupation with plot had become great enough to limit the success of any comedy without it. The demand for plot, while it had not yet in the eyes of critics supplanted the other elements of classical comedy, had certainly begun by the middle of the eighteenth century to occupy the same level of importance.

The shifting of emphasis in favor of plot might have resulted in failure had not this interest been balanced by a more attentive consideration to its construction. One is conscious of this almost from the very beginning; Destouches, for example, devoted no small amount of space to his methods of plot-construction and called attention to his efforts to obtain a logical *dénouement*. The *comédie larmoyante,* poor as some of its examples may be, necessitated a certain amount of attention to plot-construction in order to make plain to the spectator the complicated relationships of its characters. The first impulse of the eighteenth century had been to seek refuge in the confused action of the *intrigue romanesque.* The inferior results obtained by the majority of its adherents fostered in their contemporaries the idea that what was needed was not so much "une intrigue compliquée" as "une intrigue bien faite."

This vaguely defined idea was clarified by Diderot who, in his theoretical treatises, authorized the subordination of character to the element of plot and to its technical construction. In his criticism of Palissot's *Tuteurs,* Fréron had already defined the new attitude with especial regard to comedy. His criticism is important as evidence of changing values rather than as a potent factor in the direction of these values. Besides, for at least a decade, the main interests of the century were devoted to another *genre.* The old conception of comedy, however, had been definitely undermined and with the subsequent revival of interest in comedy we have the awkward but conscious application of the new values.

The definition of plot-construction as the first requisite for a successful play did not necessarily exclude from the drama subjects worthy of serious study, but it did very definitely subordinate them. Most authors of the first half of the century were noticeably indifferent to the production of comedy with a substantial *fond.* In the second half of the century authors voluntarily turned their attention to the *comédie d'intrigue* as the one comic *genre* to which the new principle was eminently adaptable. *Le Barbier de Séville* exemplified the main tendency of the epoch. In default of *fond,* the eighteenth century turned its attention to *forme* so exclusively that it became the chief aim of dramatic art.

This was the conception of comedy which the eighteenth century bequeathed to the nineteenth century. It has not been our purpose here to determine precisely how much of this conception the nineteenth century accepted, how much of it was rejected during the period which intervened between Beaumarchais and Scribe. Nevertheless if we can trust the evidence of Andrieux to which we called attention at the very beginning of this study, the first part of the nineteenth century was dominated by the ideal of the eighteenth century even as the latter had once been dominated by the classical ideal of the seventeenth century. The ideal of one age, however, cannot indefinitely dominate the ideal of another. Comedy, like any other art, depends for its very existence upon endless renewal, endless transformation, endless adaptation to the demands of a constantly changing order. The ultimate ideal of the eighteenth century coincided admirably with the spirit of the epoch which formulated it, for the eighteenth century, in contradistinction to the seventeenth, was largely concerned with the political and social welfare of man and curiously indifferent to the rational analysis of his moral struggles and the psychological study of his character. It is not strange, therefore, that the shift of emphasis which we have traced in the attitude toward comedy should have taken place in the course of the eighteenth century. In fact, it was logical, it was necessary, it was inevitable.

BIBLIOGRAPHY

A. Editions of plays with prefaces, prologues, notices, etc., of value for this study.

Andrieux, *Oeuvres,* Paris, 1822. 4 vols.
   Oeuvres, Paris, 1818–1823. 4 vols.
Autreau, *Oeuvres dramatiques,* Paris, 1749.
Beaumarchais, *Essai sur le genre dramatique sérieux,* Paris, 1767.
   Théâtre complet (ed. by G. d'Heylli and F. de Marescot), Paris, 1869–1871. 4 vols.
Boindin, *Oeuvres,* Paris, 1753. 2 vols.
Boissy, *Oeuvres,* Paris, 1738. 6 vols.
Boursault, *Esope à la cour,* Paris, 1702.
   les Fables d'Esope, Paris, 1690.
   Oeuvres choisies, Paris, 1811. 2 vols.
Bret, *Oeuvres de théâtre,* Paris, 1765.
Brueys (et Palaprat), *Théâtre,* Paris, 1735. 3 vols.
Brumoy, *le Théâtre des Grecs,* Paris, 1730. 3 vols.
Cailhava, *l'Egoïsme,* Paris, 1777.
   la Fille supposée, Paris, 1785.
   le Mariage interrompu, Paris, 1769.
   Théâtre, Paris, 1781. 2 vols.
Campistron, *Oeuvres,* Paris, 1723. 2 vols.
Collé, *l'Andrienne,* Paris, 1769.
   Théâtre de société, La Haye, Paris, 1777. 3 vols.
Descazeaux Desgranges, *la Prétendue veuve, ou l'Epoux magicien,* Paris, 1737.
Destouches, *l'Ambitieux et l'indiscrète,* Paris, 1737.
   la Fausse Agnès, Paris, 1736.
   Oeuvres de théâtre, Paris, 1745. 5 tomes in 8 vols.
   Oeuvres dramatiques, Paris, 1757. 4 vols.
   Oeuvres dramatiques, Paris, 1758. 10 vols.
Du Bruit de Charville, *l'Equivoque,* Toulouse, 1729.
Du Cerceau, *l'Enfant prodigue,* Paris, 1733.
Dufresny, *Oeuvres,* Paris, 1731. 6 vols.
Duval, *Oeuvres complètes,* Paris, 1822–1823. 9 vols.
Fagan, *l'Amitié rivale,* Paris, 1736.
   les Caractères de Thalie, Paris, 1737.
   Théâtre et autres oeuvres, Paris, 1760. 4 vols.
Fuzelier, *Momus fabuliste, ou les Nôces de Vulcain,* Paris, 1719.
   Momus fabuliste, ou les Nôces de Vulcain, Paris, 1720.
Gazon-Dourxigné, *Alzate, ou le Préjugé détruit,* La Haye, Paris, 1754.
Guyot de Merville, *le Consentement forcé,* Paris, 1738.
   les Mascarades amoureuses, Paris, 1736.
   Oeuvres de théâtre, Paris, 1766. 3 vols.
Hauteroche, *l'Amant qui ne flatte point,* Paris, 1669.
   les Apparences trompeuses, Paris, 1673.
   le Cocher, Paris, 1685.
   le Deuil, Paris, 1673.
   le Feint polonois, ou la Veuve impertinente, Lyon, 1686.
   Oeuvres, Paris, 1696.
   Oeuvres de théâtre, Paris, 1736. 3 vols.
La Chaussée, *Oeuvres,* Paris, 1777. 5 vols.

Lafont, *l'Amour vangé* (*sic*), Paris, 1713.
    Oeuvres, Amsterdam, 1746.
    les Trois frères rivaux, Paris, 1713.
La Harpe, *Oeuvres,* Paris, 1778. 6 vols.
Landois, *Sylvie,* Paris, 1742.
La Place, *le Théâtre anglois,* Londres, 1745–1748. 8 vols.
Launay (De), *Oeuvres de théâtre,* Paris, 1741.
    Oeuvres de théâtre, Paris, 1766.
    le Paresseux, Paris, 1733.
Lesage, *Théâtre espagnol,* Paris, 1700.
    Turcaret, Paris, 1709.
Linguet, *Théâtre espagnol,* Paris, 1770. 4 vols.
Marin, *Pièces de théâtre,* Paris, 1765.
Marivaux, *les Serments indiscrets,* Paris, 1732.
Moissy, *le Provincial à Paris,* Paris, 1751.
Palissot, *Oeuvres,* Liège, 1779. 7 vols.
    les Philosophes, Paris, 1760.
    les Tuteurs, Paris, 1755.
Pellegrin, *le Divorce de l'amour et de la raison, suite du Nouveau monde,*
    Paris, 1724.
    le Nouveau monde, Paris, 1723.
    le Pastor fido, Paris, 1726.
Pesselier, *l'Ecole du temps,* Paris, 1739.
    Esope au Parnasse, Paris, 1739.
    Oeuvres, Paris, 1758.
Piron, *Oeuvres,* Paris, 1758. 3 vols.
Poinsinet de Sivry, *Théâtre et oeuvres diverses,* Londres, 1764.
Poisson, Philippe, *Oeuvres,* Paris, 1743.
Regnard, *Oeuvres complètes,* Paris, 1854. 2 vols.
Rochon de Chabannes, *les Amants généreux,* Paris, 1774.
    Oeuvres (dramatiques), Paris, 1776–1786. 2 vols.
    les Valets maîtres de la maison, Paris, 1769.
Romagnesi and Riccoboni, *Théâtre italien,* Paris, 1758.
Rousseau, J. B., *le Capricieux,* Paris, 1701.
    Oeuvres, Rotterdam, 1712. 3 vols.
    Oeuvres diverses, Amsterdam, 1726. 4 tomes in 3 vols.
Sablier, *Oeuvres de M***,* Paris, 1761.
Saint-Foix, *Oeuvres de théâtre,* Paris, 1748.
    Oeuvres de théâtre, Paris, 1762.
Saurin, *Oeuvres complètes,* Paris, 1783.
Sedaine, *le Comte d'Albert,* Paris, 1787.
    le Jardinier et son seigneur, Paris, 1761.
    le Magnifique, Paris, 1761.
    Oeuvres dramatiques, Paris, 1776. 4 tomes in 2 vols.
    Oeuvres dramatiques, Paris, 1800. 5 vols.
Voisenon (?), *Oeuvres de théâtre de M***,* Paris, 1753.
Yon, *la Folie de l'amour,* Paris, 1755.
    la Métempsicose, Paris, 1753.

B. Contemporary criticism as represented by treatises on dramatic art,
anonymous pamphlets, etc.

Alletz, *les Leçons de Thalie ou le Tableau des divers ridicules que la comédie
    présente,* Paris, 1751. 2 vols.
Annales dramatiques ou Dictionnaire général des théâtres de Paris, Paris,
    1808.
Apologie du "Philosophe marié," Paris, 1727.

Appel à toutes les nations de l'Europe des jugements d'un écrivain anglais, ou Manifeste au sujet des honneurs du Pavillon entre les théâtres de Londres et de Paris, Paris, 1761.

d'Arnobat, *Observations sur la poétique française,* Amsterdam, 1769.

d'Aubignac, *Pratique du théâtre,* Paris, 1657.

Beauchamps, *Recherches sur les théâtres de France,* Paris, 1735.

Boindin, *Lettres historiques sur tous les spectacles de Paris,* Paris, 1719.

Buffier, *Suite de la grammaire française sur un plan nouveau, ou Traité philosophique et pratique de poésie,* Paris, 1728.

Cailhava, *De l'Art de la comédie,* Paris, 1772. 4 vols.

   Etudes sur Molière, ou Observations sur la vie, les moeurs, les ouvrages de cet auteur, Paris, 1802.

Charpentier, *Causes de la décadence du goût sur le théâtre,* Amsterdam, Paris, 1758. (First part dated 1768.) 2 parties en 1 vol.

Chassiron, *Réflexions sur le comique larmoyant,* Paris, 1749.

Chevrier, *Observations sur le théâtre dans lesquelles on examine avec impartialité l'état actuel des spectacles de Paris,* Paris, 1755.

Considérations sur l'art du théâtre, Genève, 1759.

Contant d'Orville, *Lettre critique sur la comédie de l'Enfant prodigue ou l'Ecole de la jeunesse,* Paris, 1737.

Diderot, *Oeuvres complètes* (ed. by J. Assézat), Paris, 1875–1877. vols. 7, 8.

Dubocage (?), *Lettre sur le théâtre anglois avec une traduction de l'Avare, comédie de Shadwell, et de la Femme de campagne, comédie de Wicherley,* n.p., 1752.

Du Perron de Castera, *Extraits de plusieurs pièces du théâtre espagnol avec des réflexions, et la traduction des endroits les plus remarquables,* Paris, 1738.

   Lettre à Monsieur Louis Riccoboni, Paris, 1737.

Encyclopédie, ou Dictionnaire raisonné des sciences, des arts, et des métiers, Lausanne, 1781–1782. 36 vols. (Articles: action, catastrophe, comédie, dénouement, drame, exposition, intrigue, *Misanthrope,* noeud, Plaute, reconnaissance, Térence, vraisemblance.)

Geoffroy, *Cours de littérature dramatique, ou Recueil par ordre de matières des Feuilletons de Geoffroy,* Paris, 1825.

La Dixmerie (Bricaire de), *les Deux âges du goût et du génie français, sous Louis XIV et sous Louis XV,* La Haye, Paris, 1769.

La Harpe, *Oeuvres,* Paris, 1778. vols. 5, 6.

Lamarche-Courmont, *Réponse aux différens écrits publiés contre la comédie des Philosophes,* n.p., 1760.

La Porte and Chamfort, *Dictionnaire dramatique contenant l'histoire du théâtre, les règles du genre dramatique . . ., avec des notices des meilleures pièces, le catalogue de tous les drames et celui de tous les auteurs dramatiques,* Paris, 1776. 3 vols.

La Porte, *Ecole de littérature, tirée de nos meilleurs écrivains,* Paris, 1764. vol. 2.

La Serre, *Mémoires sur la vie et les ouvrages de Molière,* in *Oeuvres de Molière,* Paris, 1734. vol. 1.

Les Qu'est-ce? A l'auteur de la comédie des Philosophes, n.p., 1760.

Lettre critique sur la nouvelle comédie du Philosophe marié, Paris, 1727.

Lettre sur la comédie du Méchant, n.p., n.d.

Mallet, *Principes sur la lecture des poètes,* Paris, 1745. 2 vols.

Marmontel, *Elémens de littérature,* in *Oeuvres complettes,* Paris, 1787. vols. 5–10.

   Poétique française, Paris, 1763.

Mercier, *Du Théâtre, ou Nouvel essai sur l'art dramatique,* Amsterdam, 1773.

Meslé le jeune (?), *Essai sur la comédie moderne,* Paris, 1752.

Nougaret, *De l'Art du théâtre,* Paris, 1769. 2 vols.
Nouvelle lettre écrite de Rome sur la comédie du Méchant, n.p., 1748.
Parfaict (les frères), *Dictionnaire des théâtres de Paris,* Paris, 1756. 7 vols.
  Histoire générale du théâtre français, Paris, 1734–1749. vols. 14, 15.
Pellegrin (?), *Lettre de Mlle. de C*** à Madame de N*** sur la comédie du Nouveau monde,* Paris, 1722.
Rapin, *Réflexions sur la poétique de ce temps* (2nd edition), Paris, 1675.
Réflexions critiques d'un Allemand sur la comédie de Timon le misanthrope, Paris, 1722.
Réflexions critiques sur le Philosophe marié, Paris, n.d.
Relation curieuse de tout ce qui s'est passé au Parnasse au sujet des comédies du Philosophe marié et de l'Envieux, Paris, 1727.
Riccoboni, L., *Observations sur la comédie, et sur le génie de Molière,* Paris, 1736.
le Théâtre ouvert au public, ou Traité de la tragédie et de la comédie, Paris, 1750.
Voltaire, *Dictionnaire philosophique,* Article: dramatique, in *Oeuvres complètes* (ed. by L. Moland), Paris, 1877–1885. vol. 17.
  Lettres sur les Anglais, Lettre XIX, *Sur la comédie,* 1734, in *Oeuvres complètes,* vol. 22.

C. Contemporary criticism as represented by periodicals, memoirs, literary correspondences, etc.

Aubert, *Journal des beaux-arts et des sciences,* Paris, 1768(–1774).
l'Avant-coureur, Paris, 1760–1773.
Bachaumont, *Mémoires secrets pour servir à l'histoire de la république des lettres,* Londres, 1777–1789.
Chaumeix and d'Aquin, *le Censeur hebdomadaire,* Paris, 1760–1761.
Clément, *les Cinq années littéraires, ou Nouvelles littéraires des années 1748, 1749, 1750, 1751 et 1752,* La Haye, 1754.
Collé, *Journal historique, ou Mémoires critiques et littéraires sur les ouvrages dramatiques et sur les événements les plus memorables, depuis 1748 jusqu'en 1751(–1772) inclusivement,* Paris, 1805–1807.
Desfontaines, *Observations sur les écrits modernes,* Paris, 1735–1743.
Favart, *Mémoires et correspondance littéraires, dramatiques et anecdotiques,* Paris, 1808.
Fréron, *l'Année littéraire,* Amsterdam, Paris, 1754–1775.
  Journal étranger, Paris, 1755–1756.
  Jugemens sur quelques ouvrages nouveaux, Avignon, 1744–1746.
  Lettres sur quelques écrits de ce tems, Genève, Paris, 1749–1754.
Gazette littéraire de l'Europe, Paris, 1764–1766.
Goldoni, *Mémoires de M. Goldoni pour servir à l'histoire de sa vie et à celle de son théâtre,* Paris, 1787.
Granet, *Réflexions sur les ouvrages de littérature,* Paris, 1737–1741.
Grimm, *Correspondance littéraire, philosophique et critique* (ed. by M. Tourneux), Paris, 1877. vols. 2–5.
Journal des savants, Amsterdam, Paris, 1740–1755.
La Harpe, *Correspondance littéraire, . . . depuis 1734 jusqu'à 1789,* Paris, 1801–1807.
La Porte, *Observations sur la littérature moderne,* La Haye, Amsterdam, Londres, Paris, 1749–1752.
Le Presvost d'Exmes, *le Nouveau spectateur, ou Examen des nouvelles pièces de théâtre,* Paris, 1775.
Linguet, *Journal de politique et de littérature,* Bruxelles, 1774–1778.

Mercure de France, Paris, 1720, 1735, 1738, 1739, 1745–1775.
Prévost, *le Pour et le contre,* Paris, 1733–1740.

D. Other works consulted in the course of this study.

Aristotle, *The Works of Aristotle* (tr. into English under the editorship of
    W. D. Ross), v. 11, *De Poetica,* Oxford, 1924.
Arnaud, *les Théories dramatiques au XVIIe siècle,* Paris, 1887.
Baker, G., *Dramatic Technique,* Boston, New York, 1919.
Bernardin, *la Comédie italienne et le théâtre de la Foire,* Paris, 1902.
Brunetière, *les Epoques du Théâtre Français (1636–1850),* Paris, 1896.
Burgund, E., *Die Entwicklung der Theorie der französische Schauspielkunst
    im 18. Jahrhundert bis zur Revolution,* Breslau, 1931.
Busnelli, M., *Diderot et l'Italie,* Paris, 1925.
Charavay, E., *Diderot et Fréron, documents sur les rivalités littéraires au
    XVIIIe siècle,* Paris, 1875.
Cobb, L., *Pierre-Antoine de la Place,* Paris, 1928.
Cordier, H., *Bibliographie de Beaumarchais,* Paris, 1883.
    Essai bibliographique sur les Oeuvres d'Alain-René Lesage, Paris, 1910.
Cornou, F., *Trente années de luttes contre Voltaire et les philosophes du
    XVIIIe siècle. Elie Fréron (1719–1776),* Paris, 1922.
Cru, R., *Diderot as a Disciple of English Thought,* New York, 1913.
Delafarge, D., *la Vie et l'oeuvre de Palissot,* Paris, 1912.
Des Granges, C., *Geoffroy et la critique dramatique sous le consulat et l'em-
    pire (1800–1814),* Paris, 1897.
Ducros, L., *Diderot, l'homme et l'écrivain,* Paris, 1894.
Eggli, E., *Diderot et Schiller,* in *Revue de littérature comparée,* 1921.
Font, A., *Favart, l'opéra-comique et la comédie-vaudeville aux XVIIe et
    XVIIIe siècles,* Paris, 1894.
Formentin, C., *Essai sur les origines du drame moderne en France,* Paris,
    1879.
Gaiffe, F., *le Drame en France au XVIIIe siècle,* Paris, 1910.
Günther, L., *l'Oeuvre dramatique de Sedaine,* Paris, 1908.
Hankiss, J., *Philippe Néricault Destouches,* Budapest, 1918.
Hatin, *Bibliographie historique et critique de la presse périodique française,*
    Paris, 1866.
Huzar, G., *l'Influence de l'Espagne sur le théâtre français des XVIIIe et
    XIXe siècles,* Paris, 1912.
Joannidès, *la Comédie-Française de 1680 à 1900,* Paris, 1901.
Jones, F., *Beaumarchais and Plautus. The Sources of the Barbier de Séville,*
    Chicago, 1908.
Koch, J., *Brueys und Palaprat und ihre dramatische Werke,* Leipzig, 1906.
Lacroix, P. (le Bibliophile Jacob), *Catalogue de la bibliothèque dramatique
    de M. de Soleinne,* Paris, 1843–1845. 5 vols.
Lanson, *Nivelle de La Chaussée et la comédie larmoyante,* Paris, 1903.
Larroumet, *Marivaux, sa vie et ses oeuvres,* Paris, 1882.
La Vallière, *Bibliothèque du théâtre françois depuis son origine,* Dresde, 1768.
    vol. 3.
Lemaître, *la Comédie après Molière et le théâtre de Dancourt,* Paris, 1882.
    Impressions de théâtre, IIe série, Paris, 1920.
Lenient, *la Comédie en France au XVIIIe siècle,* Paris, 1888.
Lintilhac, *Beaumarchais et ses oeuvres,* Paris, 1887.
    Histoire des théories dramatiques, in *Nouvelle Revue,* 1er mars, 1901.
    Histoire générale du théâtre en France, v. 4, *la Comédie: XVIIIe siècle,*
    Paris, n.d.

Melcher, E., *Stage Realism in France between Diderot and Antoine*, Bryn Mawr, 1928.

Moreau, P., *le Classicisme des romantiques*, Paris, 1932.

Mornet, *la Question des règles au XVIIIe siècle*, in *Revue d'histoire littéraire*, 1914.

  Madame de Grafigny, G. Noël, reviewed in *Revue d'histoire littéraire*, 1915.

Paër, A., *1784–1884. Centenaire du "Mariage de Figaro" de Caron de Beaumarchais*, Bruxelles, 1884.

Parigot, E., *Emile Augier*, Paris, 1890.

  Génie et métier, Paris, 1894.

  le Parterre au XVIIIe siècle, in *la Quinzaine*, 1er février, 1906.

Reinach, J., *Diderot*, Paris, 1894.

Rocafort, J., *les Doctrines littéraires de l'Encyclopédie ou le Romantisme des encyclopédistes*, Paris, 1890.

Rosenkrantz, K., *Diderots Leben und Werke*, Leipzig, 1866.

Sęligmann, A., *l'Influence du "Mariage de Figaro" par Beaumarchais sur la littérature française*, Prag, 1914.

Sommervogel, P., *Table méthodique des mémoires de Trévoux (1701–1775)*, Paris, 1864–1865.

Trolliet, E., *Beaumarchais, ses drames et sa théorie du drame*, in *Revue d'art dramatique*, 1887.

Van Tieghem, P., *l'Année littéraire (1754–1790) comme intermédiaire en France des littératures etrangères*, Paris, 1917.

Vial, F. and Denise, L., *Idées et doctrines littéraires du XVIIIe siècle*, Paris, 1909.

Wade, I., *The "Philosophe" in the French Drama of the Eighteenth Century*, Elliot Monographs, 18, Princeton, 1926.

Wogue, J., *J.-B.-L. Gresset, sa vie, ses oeuvres*, Paris, 1894.

Young, B., *Michel Baron, acteur et auteur dramatique*, Paris, 1905.

VITA

I, Edna Caroline Fredrick, was born in Holyoke, Massachusetts, on November 2, 1906, the daughter of George Fredrick and Ella Maria Haigh. I was prepared for college by the Holyoke High School and in September 1923 entered Mount Holyoke College where I spent four years as an undergraduate, receiving the degree of Bachelor of Arts in June 1927. During the years 1927–1929 I taught French and Latin in the High School at Millerton, New York. In September 1929 I entered Bryn Mawr College as a graduate student. I held a graduate scholarship in French in 1929–1930 and received the degree of Master of Arts in June 1930. In 1930–1931 I continued my studies at Bryn Mawr College where I held the Frances Mary Hazen Fellowship from Mount Holyoke College and the Paul Hazard Scholarship from Bryn Mawr College. I held the Mary Elizabeth Garrett European Fellowship for the year 1931–1932 and studied at the University of Paris and the Collège de France. The following year, 1932–1933, I returned to Bryn Mawr College as fellow in French.

At Bryn Mawr College I attended the graduate courses given by Dr. Eunice Morgan Schenck, Professor of French, Mrs. Grace Frank, Associate Professor of Romance Philology, Mr. Jean Canu, Associate Professor of French, Dr. Susan Ballou, Associate Professor of Latin. In Paris I attended the courses given by MM. Gaiffe, Chamard, and Michaut at the University of Paris and by M. Hazard at the Collège de France.

My preliminary oral examination for the doctorate was held on February 6, 1933. My major subject was Modern French Literature and my minor subjects, Old French Philology and Latin.

I wish to express my gratitude to Dr. Schenck of Bryn Mawr College; I have indicated my indebtedness in connection with this dissertation on page iii.